FEEL THE FEELING OF

LETTING GO IN 7 DAYS

Other books by Darla Luz

The Heart of Attention

Free yourself from stress and all inner conflict for good, creating a heart-felt life of perfection

I AM My True Self

Let go feel free, and awaken your dream life

Awakening Peace

A step-by-step guide to manifest the life you want and the world you want to see

FEEL THE FEELING OF LETTING GO IN 7 DAYS

Stop Overthinking, Improve Relationships, Live

Present, and Find True Emotional Freedom

DARLA LUZ

DEDICATION

To my dear grandson, Alfonso, the little boy who was always truthful and whose compassion for the tinniest creatures never faltered. Today, you have the qualities of those in my life who have passed on.

And to my readers… My hope is that you realize as you read the pages in this book that living at peace, with joy and love in your heart, is much easier than you ever thought possible.

CONTENTS

INTRODUCTION

I welcome you on a journey that will help you realize a changed life. I am inviting you to travel through the pages of this book where you will find only peace and calm relaxation, changing your life in unimaginable ways.

The world we live in makes everything seem far more difficult than it needs to be. We tend to believe that what we struggle with and find difficult to do is what we should value. We tend to believe that if something seems easy, it is too good to be true!

It may seem unbelievable and so unreal that to change one's life for the better all we must do is practice relaxing and find peace. And that as we come back to this peaceful space within ourselves again and again, magically, every corner of our life changes for the better.

I would like to assure you that finding a peaceful place within yourself is as true and real as the fingers on your hand!

Each of us can free our human spirit from chaos and despair. All too often we say and express how angry, unhappy, sad, disillusioned, and hopeless we feel. We express it, live it, and feel it in every cell of our physical body, undoing our life and causing astronomical damage to ourselves. More damage than we could ever imagine to our physical, mental, and emotional well-being.

Today, our mind is the most troubled and the most cluttered of disturbing thoughts and emotions it has ever been. This mind seems to be literally screaming out for the peaceful serenity that is its true spirit and nature.

In between the pages of this book, you will experience and feel the peaceful serenity and calm awareness that allows you to let go and frees you from the troubling turmoil of a difficult world.

In the same moment you feel at peace, calm and serene here, you are in that moment in the higher state of consciousness that allows you to let go of past hurtful memories, regret, unforgiveness, anxiety, jealousy, and the judgments that riddle the mind daily. And you are free of the illusion of worrisome worst-case scenarios.

I know because my own life has changed in magical ways. And I credit the consistent meditative practices I am sharing with you here because my life was not always this way.

I suffered the usual overthinking, believing every thought that crossed my mind and every painful emotion that brought a headache, stomachache, or neck pain was real and true! As a result, I experienced bouts of depression, always waiting for the next great experience to bring me happiness. I had no idea that within me waiting to be recognized was a well spring and treasure trove that could bring me heaven on earth!

Today, my overthinking has stopped, my mind is calm and present in the moment. I no longer burden my family to bring me happiness because I now know that it is all within me. The joy I feel within is profound and comes in the most mundane moments. And this joy is not reliant on the happenstance of an outer world. The peace; my more open heart of non-judgmental, unconditional love; and the increasingly deepening feeling of bliss are all proof of the success of the journey I have taken daily for more than a decade.

Please don't misunderstand, I don't mean to say that I am perfect. How I *feel* is my perfection. There are still moments when a worrisome thought enters my space. I quickly send the small-thought entity away from me where I can observe it as it diminishes in its grandiosity, and with a gentle thud watch as it turns into light, reflecting back to me a brilliant new light. I have let go and I feel free!

This is how I gently and easily dissolve thoughts that are worrisome and make me suffer. You will learn to do this here. And you will learn many more ways to diminish and dissolve thoughts that are the cause of your hardship and suffering.

In a matter of seven days to weeks, you are dissolving thoughts and emotions that no longer serve you as you realize the importance of keeping your very sacred and precious inner being free of the pollution of mental and emotional stress.

Each of us is capable of serene and peaceful feelings that you are about to experience leading you to the life you have only dreamed about.

As you begin the journey on the pages of this book, it is as if you have come to a fork in the road, a crossroads. As you turn in the right direction, you are leaving behind a daily existence of a potholed road filled with deep trenches that have made you feel stuck, hopeless, and drained of the vitality to move forward in life.

I invite you to open the gift, the infinite treasure you are about to awaken within yourself as you allow yourself to breathe deeply and comfortably until you are at peace. There is nothing else you must do. No one you must answer to. Surrender whatever you are holding on to. Give away the weighted problem, the heaviness of worry. You are free *now*, in the peaceful present moment.

The moments you spend here in tranquil peace are yours to revel in and savor because you deserve it, and because feeling *aware peace* is the most important thing to do in any given moment. Feeling peace with love in your heart is the most important thing you can do for your life!

You will learn the easiest method to elevate and uplift your mood, expanding into feelings of increasing joy and bliss.

As you practice in this book, you are letting go of the sensational headlines, news stories, and conversations. And with great relief, you are letting go of the noisy mind that holds you hostage to the narratives of past sadness and the illusion of future worry. You are learning to live in the timeless-center core of your heart, where it is easy to feel the depth of peace, joy, and unconditional love.

You now understand that no matter what happens in the outer world — whether the economy is down, inflation is on the rise, or jobs are scarce — you can create the life you've always wanted on your own because you have everything you need within. Inner peace is the new lens through which you will now see the outside world despite its scope of negative situations and occurrences.

In between the pages of this book, you are releasing the person you are not and opening to the truth of who you really are, your genuine true self.

You are realizing that you are not the person who is resentful, disheartened, saddened or hopeless. Nor are you the person who is envious, angry, enraged, irritated, annoyed, or depressed. The real and true you who has awaited your recognition is now opening to flourishing relationships, better health, more aliveness, and appreciation for life.

As you delve into your inner self of *aware peace*, you will feel the effortless quality that resides within you. *This is how you will feel the feeling of letting go.*

The magic of a changed life does not stop at the feeling of freedom from having let go of inner conflict. A magical life continues with an experience of joy that is not reliant on anything having to happen in the outer world. You are awakening a unified field of peace, wisdom, joy, infinite possibilities and potential, inspiring ideas, answers and solutions. In the heart center of yourself there are many more gifts and rewards that are yours as you ascend higher in consciousness with the practices in this book

All the peaceful, calm, and relaxed practices you will be experiencing within these pages are located together at the end of the book for easy access.

Can life really change for the better in just seven days?

If you can commit to practicing being peacefully calm, present, and in full appreciation of life for seven days, you are well on your way to letting go of the blocks that stop us from moving forward in life. If you can commit to living peacefully as you let go for seven days, then the next seven and the following seven after that will be easier!

The good news is that in the same moment you are peaceful, aware, and present, *now,* you have let go of all that has caused you suffering and hardship.

Is it possible to wake up each day with love in our heart and joy within every cell of our being? Sure, it is. Can we really let go of the worry we feel when we see and hear the chaos going on in the outer world? Yes, we can.

In this book you are realizing the vibrancy and aliveness that feeling at peace *without thinking* is awakening within you.

Are you ready to explore the depths of a vibrantly alive you, calm and centered within your heart?

Are you ready to feel relieved of the suffering and hardship of the noisy, overthinking mind?

Let's get started!

CHAPTER ONE:

DISSOLVING THE NOISY MIND

∞

When we look back, we lose our footing to move forward in life – Darla Luz

As we delve into the root cause of the noise of the overthinking mind and the overwhelming emotions the mind generates it is important to identify the triggers that keep us stuck in mental and emotional noise. We can then begin a "practice" of effortlessly dissolving it, relieving us of its relentless suffering and hardship.

Overwhelming emotions do not only come from the thinking mind. Unwanted emotions are also triggered through sensory perceptions. However, the physical body also engages with the thinking mind.

Indulging in the negative thoughts of the mind, the body produces energies like electrical charges that give us bodily discomfort whether a headache, neck pain, stomachache, or a feeling of tension that seems to never end. The physical body knows all too well the feelings of grief, sorrow, anguish, unhappiness, and heartache. It has become a routine for the physical body to indulge and produce emotions coming from negative thoughts. As if addicted to low energy, the physical body experiences these harmful emotions repeatedly, sometimes over a lifetime.

Like the mind, the physical body must be harnessed and hitched. It must be reined in just as a horse, that without guiding it masterfully, will take you untamed through perilous, risky, and unsafe landscapes. These are the effects of overthinking and its accompanying emotional stress that can contribute to a less fulfilling life.

Once you are the master, leading your life in the direction you want, your life changes. You are no longer at the whim of the capricious nature of your mind and its thoughts and emotions that trigger the physical body. You choose in which direction you want to go in life. And it is easier than you may think.

The Root Cause of the Noisy Mind

The noisy mind that overthinks is primarily due to the stress of tension-filled, worrisome thoughts. Because most illnesses are caused by stress, it is important to understand the root cause of the noisy mind and the stress it produces.

In the outer world, there are many examples in nature that mimic the stressful, incessant, relentless noise coming from the mind that leads to undesirable conditions.

When two tectonic plates suddenly slip past each other, the energy released that has built up over time and become stressed forms seismic waves that cause an earthquake. The stress-filled energy in a pressure cooker on top of a stove might explode if the temperature is not brought down. The energy of a volcano that wells up from below the earth causing stress produces an eruption.

In the same way, if we do not alleviate stress within our mental, emotional, and physical body, the result of so much energy build-up results in the negative event of a disease that has already been linked to a build-up of stress by the scientific community.

It is important to delve deeper into the core cause of stressful, tension-filled anxious worry that produces the overthinking, noisy mind.

What is your perspective of and outlook on each situation that occurs in your life?

Imagine what it would be like if you simply observed a situation from a distance in a detached manner, where you would not take in the pollution of stress, maintaining peace and calm within. The heaviness of stress would be replaced by a lightness in spirit, benefiting your health and every aspect of your life.

Can We Really Live Stress-Free?

As you commit to the practices here, know that sustaining lightness in your life is real, true, and possible.

When we are so stressed, it is difficult to *know how to* or even *to believe that we can* release stress. Because stress has been so ingrained and familiar to us through decades, and sometimes for a lifetime, we believe there is nothing we can do to release it.

Everything we experience is felt to the degree of the perspective and outlook we have on life. However, when we understand that "problems" are there to help us grow and move forward in life, a "problem" is no longer "bad" but an *opportunity to create something better.*

Keep in mind that as you commit and have an intention to let go and feel free from the stress of all inner conflict through daily meditative practices in this book, you will understand that problematic situations arise as opportunities for growth and are not something to fear. That alone will give you a new outlook on life!

Fear is the Underlying Cause of Most Negativity

Stressful thinking often comes from fear of the

unknown. When there is stress, it is difficult to focus and decide what to do about a situation in life. "What will happen to me in the future, will I stay with the job or the relationship that doesn't make me happy?" "Will I ever make enough money, or will I just get by forever?" Rumination ensues in which thoughts circle again and again, weakening our spirit and vitality for life. Out of these stressful thoughts uncertainty and a lack of control continues unabated.

We may think that we must remove ourselves from certain people or certain situations in life that trigger our stress. However, first it is important to observe how we interpret and internalize each event and occurrence in our life. While removing ourselves from negativity is the right thing to do, first we must be aware of the chain of thoughts and their emotions that trigger our stress.

The chain of thoughts that cause stress are easier to notice when we have the spaciousness in our mind that relaxation and peace create through daily meditative practices, even as we pause, take a deep breath and find peace for intervals of just seconds or moments.

Simply as you relax and find peace in each practice and meditation in this book, you will understand that dissolving the noisy, overthinking mind is much easier than you may think.

As you commit to practicing and meditating here you are on the upward spiral of consciousness. With each meditative practice you reach the core of yourself; increasingly letting go and becoming free of the noise and commotion of the small false mind.

Meditative Practice A

Reaching your peaceful center

In the following meditation you are reaching the core of yourself where there is peace as you become free and let go:

Inhale comfortably through your nose with your mouth closed. As you exhale, part your lips slightly and breathe out all tension and stress. Continue inhaling and exhaling in the same way releasing

tension and stress more and more. Tense your feet for three to four seconds then release and feel relaxation in your feet. Continue tensing for three to four seconds, and releasing your legs, thighs, torso, shoulders, and neck in the same way. Relax the muscles in your face and around your eyes, allowing your mouth to drop slightly. Put attention and focus on your breath and the peaceful calm of your body. Stay here as long as you like.

So much more is happening here than you realize. You are relieving your mental, emotional, and physical body, which leads to better health and well-being. You are present, aware... you have let go, and you are free. When you have Presence, you are living your life in the only place life truly exists, now, in this moment! When your mind is in the past or the future in worry, you are simply not living life!

As you continue practicing meditation (mindfulness) there is so much to look forward to! You will notice there is more harmony and balance in life. Life is smoother and less complicated. You attract the same peaceful flow you are generating.

In the core, rich center of yourself there is peace, wisdom, joy, infinite possibilities and potential, inspiring ideas, answers and solutions, as well as many more gifts and rewards of consciousness that await.

Meditation Creates a Spacious Mind

As we meditate, we are doing so much more than we may realize. As we meditate, we focus our attention first, on our breath which is the gateway to our vast inner self, eventually **helping us to realize who we really are**, gain intuitive insight, and expand our consciousness, opening us to infinite potential and possibilities that sit dormant within us. Through the practice of meditation, we begin to understand that we are not the fleeting thoughts and emotions coming through our mind. And we were never the past we experienced and called our own. We are so much more!

In meditation you are creating spaciousness from

thinking and making room for higher, better thoughts to come through your mind that will attract a better life. The calming peace and balance you practice as you meditate affects every corner of your life in the same way, because the peace and balance you are creating through meditation attracts the same kind of energy into your life.

Higher Consciousness Relieves All Stressful Lower Energies

The higher you go in consciousness, the less reactive you will be of stressful thoughts and emotions. Gone will be the knee-jerk reactions that caused you great hardship, putting you at risk of disease.

The higher we go on the scale of consciousness, the more health and well-being we experience. And the easiest way to begin the upward spiral of consciousness so that we can let go and become free is, again, to relax and focus on our breath, our heart, and our whole inner being. Each practice and meditation in this book will help put you on the upward spiral of higher consciousness.

You may be wondering just *how* you can relax when you are so stressed out!

Taking just a minute or two to practice here is amazingly beneficial. This is how little by little you will maintain the feeling of lightness in life as you feel free and let go rather than the weighted, heavy feeling of stress and anxiety you may be experiencing now.

Meditative Practice B

Letting Go of Stress

The following meditation will give you the feeling of lightness, easing your stress. It can be done quickly by taking just a moment from your day:

Sit in a comfortable position as you inhale through your nose. Exhale as if through a straw, imagining you are letting go of all stress that is turning into a brilliant light in front of you. Continue inhaling and exhaling in the same way until you let go, feel calm, at peace, and free of stress. Maintain the feeling of calming peace for as long as you like.

This practice helps you to let go and feel free. As you

imagine stress turning into light, you are not fighting the energy of stress but allowing it to dissolve in a kind and loving way. Keep in mind that resisting any thought or emotion of a lower energy through fighting and battling never works, because it will come back with a vengeance!

It is important to stop the overthinking that causes stress quickly. You are learning how to do this as you practice here. The thought or emotion that continues unchecked will fester and worsen, recycling, again and again, aggravating more stress, anxiety, and fear.

Meditative Practice C

Releasing Emotional Stress

When you experience a sudden stressful emotion coming from a sensory perception that triggers a memory of a stressful event, take a moment to pause:

Take a deeper breath than you normally do and inhale with your mouth closed. Then exhale with your mouth slightly open. Continue inhaling and exhaling in the same way until you are relaxed, at peace, and free of emotional stress.

Dissolving emotional stress can be done effortlessly as you take comfortable, relaxing breaths.

In an instant, the mind can take you on a chain of unwanted thoughts that keeps you stuck in emotional stress.

As you continue the practice of relaxation and peace the breath creates, the mind and body will sooner than later adapt to your new way of being.

Unwanted Thoughts Are Making You Suffer

Resisting by fighting and battling everything that is happening around us causes suffering. However, this resistance comes from the thoughts of the small mind that mostly dwells in negativity. We must not believe the thoughts coming from the false, small mind. As we dissolve the interpreter, the analyst, and the judge in our head, we are free to be our true self, the higher consciousness that we truly are and is our authentic identity. Every time you practice and meditate here you are your genuine, authentic self.

It is *presence* that protects us from all the low energies that are not aligned with the path of higher consciousness we are currently on. When we are present in the moment, we are our genuine true self. Cultivating and maintaining *Presence* will be discussed in a later chapter.

Relaxing the Mind and Body Is the Answer to Letting Go and Feeling Free of Suffering

The constant, looping thoughts that are familiar to our brain and our physical body make it difficult to simply decide to change the trajectory of the overthinking mind. If we decide we are going to try to be more positive, we will be working hard to maintain positive words and thoughts if the noisy mind is still there.

It is far better to relax the mind, bringing it into its peaceful nature through meditative practices and a daily focus of appreciating the simple and positive aspects of our life. Another way to relax the mind is by taking a walk, enjoying the beauty of nature. As we feel at one with nature, we are focused on our senses.

We are using our eyes, ears, nose, and perhaps even touch as we appreciate nature's bounty and beauty. The noisy mind has taken a backseat and become silent.

Positivity naturally takes over through the spaciousness created through practicing meditative states because less thinking and rumination makes room for higher, better thoughts, benefiting every corner of life. So that it is not necessary to "work" our way to a more positive mindset because it happens naturally and little by little as we shift our focus and attention to feeling peaceful, creating more space in our mind.

Effective Strategies to Quiet the Mind

Just as you can relieve stress calmly and peacefully as you did through meditation practice, there are things you can do in the outer world that will help you shift away from stress and bring back calm and peace into daily life.

The following are a few ways to relieve stress and the overthinking and emotional hardship that it produces in life.

The Movement of Activity Releases Stress

When the energy of stressful overthinking is running your mind and body almost any form of physical activity and movement can counteract its runaway energy.

Any activity that gets you to focus on improving your mood, sense of well-being, and a feeling of accomplishment de-activates stress. You may turn on music and practice dance steps, take a brisk walk, ride a bike, jog, take a cool, refreshing swim, or you may do the cleaning you've put off, giving you a positive feeling of accomplishment.

The flow, harmony, and balance that you create in the outer world transforms into the same harmonic balance within that is already a part of you, awaiting recognition.

As we shift our focus on something other than the overthinking, irritated mind, we benefit. Because our body, mind, and spirit are one, each influencing the

other, the flowing harmony and balance we feel physically will also affect and transfer to us mentally and
emotionally.

Appreciation Attracts Positive Energy Into Your Life

*The easiest technique, which is a secret practice you can do
to stop overthinking, elevate your mood, and evolve your
path of higher consciousness is to appreciate. Yet, many are
unaware of the immense change for the better that appreciation can have on their life. There are endless, infinite
things in life to appreciate! Creating a habit of appreciating
life in all its aspects is the best thing we can do to improve
our health, our relationships, our happiness, and even our
finances!*

*Appreciation opens our heart, creating an uplifting, ele-
vated environment in our brain, changing its chemistry for
the better. In essence, we love everything we see, hear, taste,
and touch, leaving no room for negativity.*

In full awareness, look around at your surroundings. If
you are judging and not particularly liking what you
see, begin to appreciate very generally. Look up at the

sky, even if it is cloudy. The clouds bring water to help rejuvenate and replenish, nourishing life. Surely the water that maintains our survival deserves appreciation because without water life would not be possible! The sun's light is also a life-giving, generous light. Notice how the judgmental, disapproving, critical mind is quieted as you are appreciative. This disgruntled mind has noticed how much positivity you actually have in your life!

There is an important difference between gratitude and appreciation. In the world of consciousness, having gratitude is being thankful for something that has shifted from being a struggle to something better, perhaps a turning point in life. You are now relieved of something that in the past caused you great harm. So that simply as you think of something that harmed you, however subtle it may be, you are in that moment, in its low energy.

However, remember that you are elevating your consciousness moment by moment to the highest frequency and vibration as you practice here. As you appreciate there is an expansive energetic quality of consciousness that is representative of the highest energy of love. You emanate the highest energy of love as you appreciate the feeling that comes from a loved one, a child, or a pet as you enter a room. You radiate the energy of loving appreciation as you contemplate nature's beauty and bounty. The energy of love is palpable as you appreciate the beauty and the significance of the sunrise and the sunset. Is that not love itself?

A journal is quickly filled with endless thoughts of appreciation! Simply appreciating the amazingly mysterious engineering of our physical body that does not require a need for our control is something to appreciate.

There is no doubt, no worry or fear as you appreciate. You are in a timeless moment, knowing that all will be well. Put layer upon layer of appreciative thoughts in your mind so that its expansion reaches a crescendo of joyous bliss.

Appreciation and gratitude are used interchangeably in everyday language. If you feel comfortable using the word grateful simply because you have always used it, it's perfectly fine. Remember to expand and multiply all that you are grateful for to increase the whirlwind of high vibrational joy and bliss that arises within.

Esther Hicks, author and spiritual leader describes "a vortex" as the whirlwind of energy that is captured and maintained through an experience of appreciation.

In the outer world, when we sincerely thank someone for something they have done for us, the person we are thanking would naturally want to continue to give because we have shown appreciation. The Universe, God, The All that Is, Christ Consciousness, Creation, Source energy, however we may call what we are a part of, works in the same way. As you appreciate and have gratitude with honest sincerity, you are given back more of the same that you are grateful for and appreciate daily!

Remember that our inner world is a mirror projection of the outer world we experience daily. The high energy of appreciation puts you on the path of a higher consciousness attracting many gifts and rewards in life.

When I see and hear the divisiveness between people and governments all over the world, what comes to mind is, *"If only they could focus instead on the beautiful mysteries that sustain all life in the world — the life-giving perfection of the sunrise and sunset, the amazing engineering of all lifeforms."* The shift in focus from divisiveness to the mysterious beauty in our world would change everything experienced as fear in the world toward something good. We could then move forward in the pure high vibration of awareness, peace, joy, and finally love.

This quote from Einstein comes to mind:

"The most beautiful thing we can experience is the mysterious ... He to whom the emotion is a stranger, who can no longer pause to wonder, and stand wrapped in awe … his eyes are closed." – Albert Einstein.

CHAPTER TWO:

AWARENESS IS KEY TO A

TRANSFORMED LIFE

Awareness is like the sun. When it shines on things, they are transformed — **Thich Nhat Hanh**

It is crucial to have an awareness of what you are thinking and what you are feeling in your physical body. This is the first step in letting go and feeling free. Once you commit just moments per day to the practices and meditations in this book, daily awareness will, little by little, come naturally without great effort because each practice takes you to a peaceful, relaxing, aware state. Remember that you are doing much more than you know when you go into your natural, peaceful, calm inner state of consciousness because that is who you really are, your true self and nature.

Becoming aware is simply taking a deep relaxing, peaceful breath, and there you are. Voila! You are the awareness you came into this physical existence with, free, open, and unobstructed without the relentless mind of non-stop chatter. Remember that awareness and focus on your breath is a haven, a secure and safe place.

The ultimate reward that awareness brings into our life is endless tranquility, peace, and ease of a higher, wiser consciousness. This is how relationships flourish and our experience of life is more rewarding, gratifying, and happy.

Awareness Keeps Us From Using an Experience to Escape Reality

Most people function with awareness and focus only on short spurts throughout the course of their day. They may focus for short intervals on a story they hear or read, a digital game, or a sporting event. Only to go back to the relentless chatter of a disapproving, judgmental mind. It may never cross their mind to simply sit still in the company of themselves, their inner self of depth—of profound and intense richness; a treasure trove that offers each of us true gifts and rewards in life.

This is not to say that the things that give us enjoyment have no value. They do! Life is truly about feeling joy, peace, and fulfillment. We can merge those things we enjoy, whether work or play that give us elevated emotions in the outer world and *at the same time go within and maintain the spaciousness of joyous peace and calm.* We then live in both worlds creating balance and harmony.

The beauty is that when we emerge from the stillness within, even if it is in intervals of ten to twenty seconds in the course of our day, we are happier and lighter in spirit. And when we finally express and live, moment by moment, the qualities of consciousness like wisdom, discernment, peace, and joy, we no longer depend on anything outside of ourselves to bring us happiness and joy. True success is feeling joy and being at peace without anything needing to happen in our outer world. If something exciting happens, it's okay. And if not, that's okay too. Because the infinite bounty of All that Is and Universal Source energy is within us. In any moment a peaceful joy comes effortlessly. We have everything we need within.

However, once we use the enjoyable things we do in small moments as an **escape** from ourselves, that is when we *know* we must let go so that we can feel the awareness of feeling free and find the higher consciousness that truly defines us. A practice of being aware of your true self within is the answer to every heartache, every sorrow, distress and despair! And becoming aware of your true self and identity will come about slowly but surely as you practice and meditate here.

Why Are We Not More Aware if Awareness Can Lead Us to a Rewarding and Happy Life?

Even though we find it difficult to live with the incessant, endless noise of the small mind — the put-downs

that make us feel inadequate, deficient, and lacking —
we accept its unrelenting rantings, finding moments
of escape through alcohol, over-work, games, shop-
ping, or over-indulgence in social media; whatever
takes us away from the noisy mind.

We are comfortable and familiar with the mind of
mostly negative non-stop chatter. Even though we
may realize that living aware of our inner self in
peaceful calm leads to a more rewarding and happier
life, we are so distracted by daily activities there
seems not to be enough time to simply rest fully
aware, calm, and relaxed in the present moment.
Simply being relaxed and at peace in non-thought
may seem too easy in a world we believe to be difficult and utterly complicated. We may believe that to
be truly successful in life takes blood, sweat, and
tears!

Once you've experienced being at peace and calm in
moments throughout your day, would you want to
go back to the relentless thoughts and emotions that
have caused so much stressful, tension-filled

suffering? No, of course, you would not, because it makes sense to choose peace and joy over worry, anger, regret, and any inner conflict.

So then, why are we experiencing an epidemic of feeling more stressed and anxious than ever?

Each of us came into this world with an inherent knowledge of how to create balance if we felt physically unbalanced. As a tiny infant, we innately knew that balance could be achieved by outstretching our arms to regain our harmony and balance. We innately knew where to find nurturing and nourishment. In fact, we came into this world with a mysteriously beautiful intuitive knowledge, a built-in intelligence to help us survive that is simply referred to as "instinct," which misses its mysterious quality altogether.

Slowly but surely, our society and culture gave us the rules and "laws" of how to fit into society, producing the fear of stress and anxiety within. The fear we felt further magnified a host of upsetting feelings that we came to accept as normal, because everyone was feeling what we were feeling!

We Convinced Ourselves That Feeling "Bad" Was Normal

Can you accept that feeling continuously bad is *not* normal? That you have within you now at this moment the tools to create the life you've always wanted, never again having to feel the host of mental and emotional upheavals that have become so familiar to you.

Day in and day out, we may listen to the mental havoc going on in the minds of our friends and family, and the chaotic ways of the outer world with its continuous problems. Have you ever noticed that in the outer world even if a problem in one area is resolved there is always another, sometimes greater problem to take its place.

We humans have lived as if lack, limitation, and continuous upheaval in our third-dimensional earth-plane lives are normal. We have resigned ourselves to accept constant upsetting disturbances because it is what we have always experienced.

It is familiarity that has kept us stuck in the small mind of mental and emotional upheaval. Believe it or not, being familiar and feeling comfortable with daily upset keeps us hopelessly stuck in it.

Meditative Practice D

Becoming Familiar With Your True Nature and Identity

As we practice meditation, or what is referred to as mindfulness, we are practicing becoming familiar with our inner being, the space within ourselves, our identity and true nature. This is the space within us that through cultivation, nurturing, and finally expressing it, moment by moment, is what leads to letting go and freeing us so that we can live a happier, more rewarding life.

In the following practice, you are becoming *familiar* with your inner self, who you really are, your true self and true nature.

Take a few relaxing breaths until you feel calm, re-laxed, and at peace. Put *aware* focus on your breath. As you take a few focused, relaxing breaths, notice the mind quiets down when you are aware and fo-cused. If your mind wanders, bring it back again and again to an aware focus on your breath. Con-tinue until you feel completely relaxed and at peace.

As you practice a meditative state of awareness and focus on your inner self and breath, you have let go of anger, hopelessness, sadness, regret, fear, tension, and stress.

You may do this mindfulness meditative practice daily for five to ten minutes as you begin, increasing the practice to fifteen minutes or more as you become more and more familiar and comfortable with the spaciousness within you.

Meditation Helps You Live Present and Aware

Can you understand the great advantage of living now, in the present moment, where there is no sad-ness or fear. Remember that the moment we are pre-sent, we have let go and we are free. More will be discussed in a later chapter on the great value of living present and fully aware.

You will notice, as I do, that when you get into the habit of meditative practice, even for just five minutes in the morning, your day will be smoother, more balanced and harmonious.

This is the space that will help you become more aware. *Awareness is powerful.* Every moment you spend in awareness of your breath, an important part of your inner being, is a powerful moment because you are becoming familiar with your true and genuine Self to be expressed and lived with awareness, peace, and a quiet mind. Little by little your awareness will include your surroundings and everything that occurs in your daily life as you maintain yourself free of any pollution coming from the outer world. You are learning here how to protect yourself from the pollution of the low energy of an outer world. In fact, there will come a time when you become so aware daily that there will be no need to meditate because you are living moment by moment in a meditative state. You are then aware and aligned with Consciousness Itself, the All that Is, and Source energy.

Speak Only Powerful Words After I AM

Awareness and self-observation are the key to letting go of negativity. When we are not conscious and aware of our thoughts and emotions, we do not know why we are feeling emotionally down. We may not even be able to describe the endless list of words in our vocabulary that describe suffering.

Sometimes we may be able to reveal how we feel by adding a detrimental word. We may say "I am ... depressed, angry, sad, miserable, or worried." In those moments, we identify with emotions and feelings that are not who we are. We identify, instead, with the false ego self that relentlessly sends us thoughts and images about past sadness or future worry. An image of something we experienced as sad in the past crosses our mind, again and again, disheartening and depressing our spirit. Or an image of a worst-case scenario happening in the future of a situation we may be worrying about makes its way into our mind repeatedly causing fear, dread, and tension. Keep in mind that all low energy thoughts and emotions coming from past turmoil as well as future fear are detrimental to our health and well-being.

The word "I" is one we hear most often and take in as very natural. However, this "I" comes all too often from the ego of a lesser, low energy that forms the thoughts and emotions that cause us great harm. The word "I" is probably the most used word around the world. When the false ego has taken over, it is predominant and holds a tighter and tighter grip on us the more we indulge in its negativity. Words like "I'm unhappy, I'm depressed, I'm angry" produce a low energy that affects not only us, but others. Remember that everything is energy and goes out into the environment, including the words we speak.

Imagine the millions of times you may have inadvertently said I am…angry, depressed, sad; all negative things about yourself, and how detrimental it has been to your health and well-being!

When we become aware of an emotion that is bringing us down, it is best to refer to how we feel by saying aloud or silently, "I feel angry" or "I feel sad." By using the words "I feel" instead of "I am," we are in that moment acknowledging and detaching from the emotional state of the false self that we are beginning to recognize is not who we are. Little by little we are realizing we are not the thoughts and emotions that come from the noisy, agitated mind of the false self.

Once you realize you are not your thoughts and emotions—and you *will* as you practice here—you make it a priority to be aware of what you are thinking. Only then can you shift easily and purposefully to better, higher thoughts that make you feel good, improving your life in amazing ways. Awareness changes your life, always in a good way!

Remember that you are not the thoughts and emotions that are transient, fleeting, short-lived, and temporary. You are a vast, infinite Being connected to a powerful Universal Source energy, far removed from the finite, limited nature of circling, looping thoughts and emotions. You are the clear, vast sky behind the transient, stormy clouds. And you have the depth of the ocean in calm peaceful tranquility. You are not on the stormy ocean surface. You have depth!

Any thoughts or emotions that have produced hardship and suffering are false because the truth is you are a powerful being connected to Universal Source Energy who can move your life in the direction you want!

Positive Affirmations Beginning With I Am Are Powerful!

"I am …" followed by positive words create intention, presence, awareness, and a life that is being lived purposefully and powerfully. In the moment you affirm "I am positive, I am confident, I am loving and kind—any positive description—the subconscious mind is listening. And because it does not discern, it takes everything in as truth. The more you practice positive affirmation, you create an environment around you and others that is an uplifting, positively charged energy.

In a matter of weeks and months, negativity can begin to dissolve when you replace negativity with positive, affirmed words that turn into positive thoughts about yourself.

The "I" that you are practicing here comes from a depth, a Divine that never produces suffering. You will feel the energies of peace, joy, compassion, and love as you affirm who you really are. You are at the same time living present, now, in this moment. There is never suffering or hardship as you live from the core of your inner being, purposefully living in truth and positivity; fully aware, focused, and at peace *now*, in this moment.

It is important to be aware of what our emotional energy field feels like. Because without awareness, unwanted thoughts and emotions coming from the small, false self will take over

Meditative Practice E

Softening and Quieting the Mind

Keep in mind that even as you practice awareness and meditation, you may become aware of unhelpful thoughts that trigger emotions like sadness, anger, anxiety, or stress. It does not mean that you are failing as you practice awareness. Awareness takes consistency and commitment. Accept the unhelpful thoughts without battle or fight, and simply continue a practice of a focused, relaxed, calm peace.

Relax as you inhale and exhale comfortably focusing on your breath so that your mind softens and quiets down. As you become aware of a thought coming through, say, "next thought please," and simply wait for the next thought. You will notice that the mind becomes unbelievably quiet!

If you have ever experienced hearing something in the middle of the night that awakens you, you become very alert and aware waiting for the next sound.

Hopefully it will all turn out okay, but you can see how waiting for the next thought, the next sound brings about an alert, silent awareness.

When you are aware, the small mind quiets, creating a pathway to a more spacious mind. You have decluttered your mind so that there is more room for intuitive inspiration, discernment, and higher, wiser thoughts.

Awareness is everything! It is the key to a more fulfilling and happy life because awareness helps you feel the freedom that letting go gives you.

Pause Often to Feel How You Feel

Becoming aware of how you feel moment to moment is a good way to practice awareness. Be the guardian, the witness, and the observer of every emotional feeling that produces suffering. Be the protector of your inner self!

Stop often during your day to monitor how you are feeling. Imagine a world in which we could not feel our feelings. An emotional feeling that brings us down producing sadness, anger, or hopelessness harms us mentally, emotionally, and physically. As we feel a feeling that harms us mentally, emotionally, and physically, we are protected because it is an indicator—a needle—alerting us to shift a feeling to a higher, more elevated feeling so that we are not harmed. Think of a feeling as a friend guiding you in the right and best direction toward the life you have always wanted.

Remember that your breath alleviates, eases, and lightens any burden you carry immediately. It is the gateway into the self that brings many rewards and gifts to life.

All too often we allow emotions—like electrical charges—from thoughts, to take us over, causing un-relenting sadness, anger, regret, disheartenment, re-sentment, disillusionment, hopelessness, or any inner conflict. Sometimes a distressing feeling comes from our sensory perceptions that cause an emotional trig-ger which produces a feeling that depresses or sad-dens, leaving us in disharmony physically, mentally, and emotionally.

Each of our senses can trigger a distressing, emotional response. The sound of a siren may trigger an un-pleasant memory we experienced as a child, produc-ing a fearful emotional response. The smell of lotion or perfume may trigger a sad memory of the loss of a loved one. We may see, taste, or touch something that triggers a range of emotions, some sad, some reflective. Remember that we are not in control when we are at the whim of the small mind, with its impulsive and capricious nature. The goal is to be the guardian of our very sacred, real, and true inner *Being*.

CHAPTER THREE:

EMBRACING EMOTIONAL

AWARENESS

❧❦

We let go of overwhelming emotions by feeling
*them wholly and completely – **Darla Luz***

It is important to learn to self-regulate and express emotional awareness because, primarily, it frees us and helps us to let go, restoring our health and well-being. Emotions are generated from thoughts and sensory perceptions filtering through to our nervous system and body. These emotions are expressed through facial gestures, physical activities, and words, if overwhelming, lashing and hurtful ones.

Many people suppress their emotions, continually monitoring them so that they do not come to the surface where they are expressed. Other people re-press their emotions, not even realizing they feel the emotion.

Suppressing and repressing our emotions blocks and hinders our ability to let go and feel free. For this reason, it is important to understand their roots and learn how to gently remove unwanted emotions without fighting them. We can then freely and openly express ourselves without suppression or repression.

Meditative Practice F

Dissolving Overwhelming Emotions By Not Fighting Them

Remember that through embracing and accepting un-wanted emotions and allowing them to flow without fighting them is how we dissolve them. We can then more easily find our way to the rich center within.

In the following practice, as soon as you feel the emotional energy charge of an overwhelming emotion, allow the emotion to pass through you, feeling its intensity as it dissolves:

Take slightly deeper comfortable breaths, accepting and allowing only the energy of emotion (not the thought) no matter how intense. Feel the intensity of the emotion, no matter how strong, until the energy of the emotion subsides. Revel in the tranquil peace as you continue focusing on your slowed down, easy breaths.

Feeling and allowing the emotion to pass through you, as you just did, is accepting the emotion, not fighting it. You are learning to feel emotion rather than suppressing or repressing it. You are allowing, accepting, and embracing an unwanted emotion to pass through you, so that little by little the overwhelming emotion will get weaker, lose its momentum, and subside altogether, never to bother you again.

You will learn that the path to release all inner conflict is within you as you acknowledge and accept that which causes hardship and suffering. It does not mean that through acceptance you allow it to stay. Rather, it means you do not resist, battle, and fight what you want to be dissolved. You are dissolving and letting go, easily and effortlessly, an emotion that has kept you in an unrelenting grip, no matter how long you have experienced it.

Do this practice each time you feel an overwhelming emotion. The energy of the emotion can pass through your heart, your chest, or your whole body, whichever feels right to you.

As We Surrender, We Let Go

As we allow an emotion to "pass through," we surrender easily and without effort. We are not harming or causing hardship and suffering within. We accept a situation or an emotion that would normally be a burden of worry, unease, or agitation, to simply *be*, without trying to change it.

In our daily language, the word surrender has a negative connotation. We may think of surrender as being submissive, allowing someone else to be the "winner."

We may not like the word surrender, yet in a spiritual

sense, to surrender leads us onto a path of a better, more fulfilled, and happier life. As we surrender, we no longer suffer the agonies of anger, rage, revenge, or malice. Nor do we feel emotionally resentful, jealous, disheartened, regretful, remorseful, or guilty.

Yet, our logical left brain says we need to give attention to our emotions because the way we *feel*, after all, is very real and unmistakable. Logically, it reasons, if we feel anger, rage, remorse, or guilt, there is no doubt that it is real.

However, remember that as we surrender, we are transcending the mind and going beyond to a powerful place within. We are going above and beyond the logic of the false, small mind. Remember each of us is not the small mind that indulges in negativity. Each practice you are doing here is leading you to the best and finest version of yourself, your true identity.

When we surrender there are only feelings of peace, which are powerful in themselves. While it is true that surrendering does not happen overnight, we are led little by little to feeling peacefully surrendered more often. And, as we practice, slowly but surely, we realize the gift of surrendering, because life becomes calmer and more peaceful. Doesn't it make sense that it is surrender that we want to cultivate and develop and not continue the emotional upheaval we have become all too familiar with and believe to be normal.

Emotional Stress Produces Great Havoc in Life

Remember that emotional stress that produces feelings and emotions of anxiety, fear, and tension is the cause of great havoc, not only in our relationships and how we look at life, but to our health and well-being as well. We may think that the emotion of stress is a normal part of life. However, precautions must be taken to protect ourselves from the destructive ways of emotional stress. Keep in mind that stress has been scientifically linked to disease.

Surrendering, then, is allowing yourself to simply *Be* in the feeling state of peace, wisdom, clarity, and balance, free of dis-ease.

Emotional awareness is the foundation and corner-stone of "emotional intelligence." In the wisdom, balance, and purity of consciousness, which *is* awareness, we can now respond to the upheaval in daily life that is considered normal. We can respond with clarity, wisdom, and integrity, without malice and judgment.

Be Aware of How You Feel Throughout the Day

Becoming aware of our emotions is crucial. Stop often to feel your emotions. A good time to do this is as you finish a task and before you start another. Or you might consider setting a timer to remind you to feel what mood you are in.

Remember that feelings are like indicators warning you to elevate your mood to a higher level. When you begin to take the time to be aware of your emotional state, you are taking control of your life, leading it in the direction you want. And the more you practice elevating your emotions to a higher consciousness of wisdom, peace, and joy, the more quickly you will be out from under the heaviness of an emotion you do not want. You are elevating to a higher consciousness as you practice and meditate daily, even for just moments out of your day.

As We Acknowledge Emotions, We Let Go of Suppression and Repression

As you become aware of a weighted, lower mood, acknowledge the emotion by describing it. If you are feeling depressed, say "I *feel* depressed," or if you are feeling sad say, "I *feel* sad." Even if you are feeling happy or great, acknowledge that too. Whatever you feel, verbalize it out loud. There have been studies showing that saying how we feel whether out loud or to ourselves diminishes the weight and intensity of a heavy, emotional feeling. You are not indulging in the emotion, you are simply recognizing that the emotion is coming through, neither fighting it nor resisting it. However, you are acknowledging all emotional states to help you let go of suppression or repression. Using words to describe how you feel is a good way to learn to express emotions.

Remember that as you acknowledge how you feel, by saying *I feel* rather than *I am*, you are simultaneously detaching from the false identity of the small self, and identifying with who you really are, your true nature and true self. It is a small but beneficial movement toward the self, where you will reap endless gifts and rewards.

Verbalizing how you feel works in the same way as when you reveal to a close friend or loved one how you are feeling. You feel better as you talk about how you feel. You take weight off your chest even if someone is just listening without giving feedback. And as you hear the words you speak, it is even possible to understand the cause of your unwanted feelings and emotions and suddenly have insight into how whatever you are going through can be resolved.

Another way we learn to express emotions is through writing down and describing the emotional feeling, such as through journaling.

We can also imagine ourselves expressing our emotions wisely. If there is anger, for instance, we might imagine ourselves calmly explaining the reason for our anger to someone we have anger towards. And we might imagine the person understanding and giving us calm feedback helping to resolve our anger.

However, keep in mind that each time we imagine ourselves calm, we *will* eventually *be* calm. *Only then can we express how we feel with the person we have anger toward.* With patience, commitment, and intention to do the meditative practices here, calmness rather than anger will be our new expression.

We are self-regulating as we take charge of our emotions, letting go and freeing ourselves of suppressing or repressing emotions.

Meditative Rest Creates Emotional Awareness

A daily practice of meditation can also help you be more emotionally aware and alleviate unwanted emotions causing harm. There is no doubt that as you focus on your breath while you meditate and reach a deep, calm, at peace state, the more it helps you physically, mentally, and emotionally. It is a restful state away from the stress and anxiety of emotions. Meditation helps you create space between thoughts and the emotions that thoughts generate.

The mind gains clarity because the clutter of unwanted thoughts and emotions is no longer there. In spacious clarity, new insights and inspired ideas come through seemingly effortlessly to help you solve a problem.

I experienced spacious clarity in my own life when I contemplated a beautiful lake scene framed by a snow-capped mountain. In a couple of months something amazing happened. I felt "pulled" to a destination to find the solution to my problem, which I wrote about in my first book, *The Heart of Attention*. I received the perfect solution to my problem which had produced a lot of stress in my life. This is a good example of what happens when we surrender and let go! My consciousness was simply at rest in non-thought, fully surrendered in peaceful, pleasurable moments.

Physical Movement Calms Emotions

Movement is a great elixir for an emotion that weighs us down. The exhilaration of basketball, soccer, or tennis revitalizes our spirit and helps us shift our breathing from the shallowness of emotional fear and tension to a breath of more depth and power. Running, walking, hiking, and biking are methods of reducing stress because they support a connection to nature, putting us in a positive frame of mind, benefiting us both mentally and emotionally. And when we engage in the movements of dancing or skating, we are "in the flow," aligned with and surrendered into the natural harmony, balance, creativity, joy, and effortlessness of a Universal Source energy.

Being an Observer Is the Realization of Your True, Greater Self in Full Awareness

Thoughts and the emotions they produce can be observed at a distance away from you. As you observe your thoughts and emotions from a distance, you have a new realization and understanding that thoughts are not who you are. The thoughts or emotions are over "there," while you remain "here."

As an observer, you realize that you are not the unwanted thoughts and emotions that envelop your body causing harmful electrical-like charges. A transformation takes place because you no longer indulge in unwanted thoughts and emotions, relieving you of the harm they once caused mentally, emotionally, and physically. You are free because you have let go and are in full mastery of the life you want.

You realize that you do not need thoughts, and the emotions thoughts produce, to feel alive because you *feel* just as alive, and even more so, without thinking. Inner peace and presence are your true identity, and you no longer identify with the unwanted emotions that once ruled your life.

As an observer you are in full acknowledgement and acceptance of an emotion. As you accept an unwanted emotion, you are not resisting or fighting it. There is neither judgment, resentment, nor any ill will as you create distance between you and an unwanted thought or emotion. You are the guard and protector of your inner peace, a most important goal in life.

Notice the peace, silence, and freedom as you observe a thought from a distance.

As you observe from a distance, you realize that you are not your unwanted thoughts or emotions, which is an important part of letting go and feeling free. You are here and the unwanted thought or emotion is over there away from you. You are discovering your true power through presence and awareness.

As you observe a thought, there is no resistance, fight, battle or judgment. An unwanted thought does not produce suffering or hardship when you do not resist by fighting it. The small false ego mind softens and does not fight back because there is no resistance on your part.

Being an observer of thoughts is a powerful way to detach and let go of bothersome thoughts and the emotions that are supercharged by these unwanted thoughts because you are at peace and in non-resistance when you simply observe your thoughts.

Meditative Practice G

Detaching As You Observe An Overwhelming Thought

In the following practice, you are accepting and allowing, not fighting, and, at the same time, you are disidentifying with an unwanted thought and its emotion:

As soon as you become aware of an unwanted thought imagine it in front of you and at least ten feet away. You have detached from the thought and its emotion, and you are aware and present as you simply observe the thought from a distance. Observe it for as long as you like, imagining the thought or emotion transforming into light. In this moment you too, have transformed. You are aware and present. Revel in the peace and the freedom you feel as you let go.

A lot more than you may realize is happening in the moment you simply observe a thought from a distance.

Keep in mind that as soon as you are calm, simply observing thoughts and their emotions, allowing them to come and go, you have let go and you are free.

Little by little you begin to realize you do not have to endure the high cost and detriment to your mental and emotional well-being that come from negative thoughts and their supercharged emotions. Instead, as we keep our thoughts and feelings elevated with the positive, wise thoughts of consciousness, we benefit not only ourselves but those around us.

This is not only because the energy we put into the environment is magnetic and contagious, but also because our entire life transforms into positive, uplifting expressions when we detach from the mind that causes harm. When we let go and feel free as we detach from what harms, there is more joy, peace, and enthusiasm in our life. With more positivity and lightness coming from our inner being, our perspective of life changes, creating flourishing relationships and benefiting every corner of our life.

Observing a Situation, Thought, or Emotion

As you observe an unwanted thought, emotion, or a situation, you are one with the energy of your higher consciousness. Universal Consciousness is not dualistic, polarized, or separate as energy is in our third-dimensional world. However, because we are a part of Universal Consciousness, we and all life are One. We are integrated in compassion, integrity, and unconditional love. And it is a safe and secure place in which we are never harmed physically, mentally, or emotionally.

Being an observer is not easy, at first. With practice observing a thought from a distance and away from you will be easier. Keep in mind that the more practice you gain as you do mindfulness meditation, the more aware, alert, and spacious you will be, making it easier to become an observer.

As an observer, you acknowledge and accept the

thought or emotion with no fight or battle. You experience no frustration, annoyance, or disturbance. It is as if you have in loving kindness turned the unwanted thought, emotion, or situation into its highest form, light. You have, in integrity, given the thought or situation its highest form. And because you have surrendered it in light, you are free, and you have let go of the burden you were carrying, knowing that all will be well.

This is the science-backed subject-object principle that I have written about in my prior books. It simply states that as a subject (you) observes an object (the thought, emotion, or situation) both subject and object change.

You now have the tools to either distance yourself from an emotion or thought, or to allow the energy of the overwhelming thought or emotion to pass through you. However, at first it may be difficult to do either when you are caught off guard and an overwhelming emotion comes through.

For this reason, it is important to be aware and

understand that the constant, insistent chatter of the small false mind is not who we are and is the cause of the emotional low energies that produce hardship and suffering in life.

With this understanding you are more ready and calm when emotions arise. *Know* that with practice and commitment, in time, overwhelming emotions will subside and dissolve altogether.

You might find it easier to observe thoughts and emotions by imagining a symbol. Having a symbol in your imagination that represents a thought makes it easier to quickly detach and distance an unwanted thought or emotion. A symbol might be of an animal you'd like to tame, just as you are taming the thinking mind, and the physical body that is guided by the thinking mind.

As you practice appreciation, positive affirmations, meditation, and observing thoughts, you are protecting your energy from outside influences. You are guarding your inner space from the pollution of energy that no longer serves you.

Ensuring Healthy Relationships

Feelings have replaced emotions, and they are non-judgmental and softer, and not unconsciously reactionary like emotions. Emotions *can* help us become more aware simply through the strength of their reactionary triggers that are physically overwhelming. However, through the realization and understanding that we are not the thoughts and emotions that have caused us hardship, we are, more and more, *feeling* what really matters: life's vibrant, energetic beauty all around us.

As you follow the path of higher consciousness, it is important to ensure mental, emotional, and physical well-being. And you are doing that as you practice here. It is crucial to protect your inner peace and personal space as you maintain healthy relationships with others.

As we gain higher consciousness, we naturally steer through different kinds of energies in the outer world. We no longer build fences or divisions that separate us from others. Instead, the spiritual journey is about creating spacious awareness, as we grow while protecting our personal energy and well-being from low energies in a non-combative way. In this way, we can stay neutral and have a more positive outlook on life.

We can then move forward in loving kindness. As a result, we embrace all life without judgment or criticism, greatly contributing to an integrated life, having realized our interconnectedness with others.

While this may seem like a challenge to accomplish, remember that consciousness is effortless. Simply as you commit to the practices here, meditating for a few minutes daily, and elevating your inner energy through appreciative thoughts, you will experience a new way of being in weeks or months! You will feel calmer, freer, and you will *feel the freedom of letting go.*

As you continue the path to higher consciousness just as you are doing here, your higher vibrational energy levels cannot be impacted by others nor by situations.

You can now, with little effort, say no to others and

events that do not resonate with your values and ideals. And because you are in the upward spiral of a higher consciousness there is only benevolence and humanity. You can now acknowledge your limits and needs with direct words that are kind and firm.

In maintaining emotional awareness, through the many ways you have learned here, you are protecting yourself from being carried away by external energies that no longer serve you. And you are gaining self-esteem, self-care, and self-respect.

Thank you for making it this far!

I greatly appreciate the time you took to read my book. It means a lot to me, and I hope you have been helped on your journey to find peace and finally let go and feel freer.

If you have a minute, it will mean the world to me to read your honest feedback on Amazon.

Your review does wonders for the book and will help me offer the book to others who can be helped by reading it.

To leave a review, go to the sales page where you purchased the book on Amazon, scroll to the bottom where the reviews are, and on the left side you will see **'review this product'** and click on 'write a customer review.'

Thank you!

CHAPTER FOUR:
LETTING GO OF OVER
ATTACHMENT

*Slowing down our breath helps us to let go of the
suffering of over attachment – **Darla Luz***

The care, attention, and support we experience early
in our life influences the attachments we form
throughout our lives, often impacting our health and
well-being. Because emotional attachment often leads
to suffering, there is a need to reflect on our experience in early life, to learn to let go of over-attachment,
and to nurture a sense of freedom and inner peace.

 The good news is you are already practicing a sense
of freedom, inner peace, and letting go leading to
healthier, enriching relationships.

While we are practicing awareness and being present in the moment, we are realizing the gift of awareness and presence. Because they are free of worry about what the future holds and free of the past that no longer exists and, therefore, is no longer relevant.

However, we can go back to our childhood and, for only a moment, remember the pattern we adopted to ensure ourselves of the best care and support from a caregiver, whether a parent, grandparent, or guardian.

Our Natural Human Need for the Survival of Our Species

A British psychoanalyst, Dr. John Bowlby, in the 1940's recognized our human innate need for attachment. In his research, he hypothesized that attachment is an inherent human need within each of us to maintain the very survival of our species.

His reasoning established that an "unhealthy" human attachment should not be considered a degraded emotional state but approached with 'curiosity and respect.'

He recognized a child's need for attention and support as he watched children play. When the child experienced a scary dog, the child ran to a caregiver for comforting support, and after feeling renewed, returned to play.

He found that the comfort and support we receive from a caregiver becomes an important part of our development that helps us ease back into a comfortable, renewed focus on play, work, or any activity — changing our chemistry within and helping us to thrive and learn more effortlessly.

Feeling Safe and Secure Enables Learning and Growth

Dr. Bowlby found that safety enables learning. So, the conclusion is that we all need a place to be safe and a place for growth.

If we experienced a caregiver who was supportive but unresponsive we may have learned to suppress our feelings, carefully monitoring them to avoid exposing ourselves to the pain and suffering of rejection and betrayal.

On the other hand, if we had a caregiver who was neither supportive nor responsive we may have learned to anxiously cry out for our needs, magnifying the suffering of rejection and betrayal. And whatever response we receive, that kind of response is taken into adulthood.

Yet, it really does not matter what we experienced in childhood, because it is our perspective of life that matters most. So that what we experience is not set for life. You are gaining a new perspective on life as you commit to practicing here.

Let's say that two people form a relationship, one who anxiously magnifies their need for attachment and the other who suppresses their feelings. Which of the two would be considered to have an "unhealthy" attachment and called "needy?"

And would a need for loving support be considered wrong?

According to Dr. Bowlby, each of us came into this life experience with an inherent need for caring support because it sustains the survival of our human species, and because feeling loved and supported helps us evolve and grow.

Dr. Bowlby held that we all need loving care and support. The attachment to our caregiver is so deeply embedded, not only in our human species, but in all species.

The couple who forms a relationship where one is anxiously wanting loving support from the partner who suppresses their feelings are stuck in an emotional, impassive tug of war.

However, according to psychologist Susan Johnson who has studied relationships in which one partner is the pursuer and the other the avoidant, discovered a hidden thread, a storyline that binds them.

It is the depth of our inner self — our core and heart — that binds each of us, no matter who we are or where we come from. These are the precious feelings that connect two people.

When the crying and the rejection stop, then there can

be a coming together with compassion and under-standing. They can then understand that with support and caring there is learning and growth.

As our reactions soften our curiosity grows and learning is enabled.

Meditative Practice H

Feeling Safe and Secure By Slowing Down Your Breath

Remember that all behavior makes sense even when you experience an "unhealthy" over attachment. The following breathing practice will calm you.

The following is yet another way to dissolve an overwhelming feeling. In this case, an overwhelming feeling of attachment.

Put *aware focus* on a slightly deeper inhalation than normal with your mouth closed. And, as you exhale, part your lips slightly and imagine you are slowly breathing out the unwanted emotions causing suffering. Continue until you feel completely at peace.

As you do this, your mind and body slow down, causing rampant emotions to slow, and relieving you as you let go of the emotions that are detrimental to your health and well-being. The slowing-down effect of taking deep slow breaths activates your internal mechanism of feeling safe and secure.

Our heart rate slows, and our reactionary impulse softens, giving us a safe place to open, to be vulnerable.

Staying Solidly on the Path of Higher Consciousness

Remember that every time you practice a state of slowing down to peaceful, good feelings, you are on the path of the upward spiral to higher consciousness.

Higher Consciousness does not waiver. It is eternal and endless. Higher consciousness does not rely on what is happening "out there." Higher consciousness comes naturally, without effort from the peaceful tranquility of our inner being and it is available moment by moment, and not only in short intervals. As we gain higher consciousness, we can neutralize and detach from emotions and continue to sustain peace easily and effortlessly.

Peace, calm, and tranquil joy, continuous and sustained, that comes from higher consciousness is what we deserve!

As we continue the path of an upward spiral toward higher consciousness, we begin the journey of knowing who we are: a being who derives its sense of comfort and support through the self. Our innate need for support, consolation, and reassurance shifts as we realize a deeper, peaceful, unconditional love and joy that does not rely on anything that has to happen in the outside world. We are no longer in the survival mode that seemed needed in this physical existence. We can maneuver life in an easier more effortless way in higher consciousness.

Just How Do We Stay Neutral and Detached

As we gain higher consciousness, if a "bad" emotional feeling is triggered it does not affect us because we can detach from it and "see" it at a distance where we can observe it. Or we can observe the feeling of unwanted emotions as we rest and relax. In this way, we dissolve an attachment as we protect ourselves from the pollution of a "bad" emotional feeling. Nothing is bad in the neutral state of consciousness. It is our perspective, our outlook on life, that produces an experience that is either good or bad.

Just as we have already discussed being the observer in a prior chapter, it will also be made mention here to bring about a healthy detachment from overwhelming emotions of attachment.

Meditative Practice I

A Good Way to Detach Is in Pure Relaxation, Feeling Emotions Coming Through and Dissolving

As an observer you are detached from emotions of attachment in an easy and effortless way. There is no fight or battle. You are in peaceful tranquility as the emotions of attachment dissolve.

Any form of attachment that makes us feel bad is something we must dissolve.

In the following practice you are in a state of pure relaxation as you observe and feel emotions coming through, softening and dissolving.

Take a deeper, comfortable breath and exhale unwanted emotions of attachment. Continue taking comfortable breaths and exhaling emotions of attachment until you feel safe, calm and secure. As you continue, take comfortable breaths and at the same time, put awareness on your entire body from your head to your toes. As you feel safe and secure, and at peace, is there an uncomfortable feeling someplace in your body? If so, feel it and allow it to slowly dissolve. As you feel each emotion that is uncomfortable, stay with each one, until each subsides and dissolves.

Remember that as you feel safe and secure, you become open. Your heart opens to compassion and love, and you feel safe enough to be vulnerable. You can now speak your feelings openly and honestly and without fear.

When the mind is at peace, you are luxuriating in the

state of higher consciousness without need to interpret or analyze. Higher consciousness is the entry point to feeling safe, secure, peaceful joy, and bliss. The real and true essence is your true self simply *being,* simply feeling in the centered, open heart of yourself in this moment.

That is where detachment from an "emotional over attachment" begins, and love emerges.

Remember, once we attach to form, producing an emotional over attachment, be it a person or something material that we may have lost and is the cause of suffering, we are at the level of the false ego self.

Remember that love is at the level of *being.* When we feel safe, alive, and vibrant, tuned into the truth of our being, we can feel the true essence of another allowing love to emerge.

And the ability to be vulnerable as we feel safe is at the heart of every successful, intimate relationship.

CHAPTER FIVE:

CULTIVATING SELF-COMPASSION

AND SELF-LOVE

∞

*"All you really need to do is accept this moment fully. You are then at ease in the here and now and at ease with yourself." – **Eckhart Tolle***

A relationship with ourselves is something we may not have thought about or even considered important. However, simply sitting in quietude listening to our breath promotes self-love and is an important part of letting go, feeling free and being our Greater, genuine self. You will be guided here to nurture and develop a kind relationship with yourself.

We have already discussed the importance of knowing who you are as your true, genuine self. A realization of your true identity will come about naturally as you practice here. And it is knowing who you are that will, primarily, help you let go and feel free.

What if I told you that you are already cultivating self-love through the meditations and practices you have done here. That every time you relax and are at peace with yourself, you gain self-compassion, self-love, self-esteem, and self-respect.

You can acquire self-love in a much easier way than you may believe. You will do it comfortably and without great effort here.

The consistent practice you are doing here of mindfulness meditation, affirmations, as well as the positive practices of appreciation and gratitude is awakening you to who you genuinely are. There is no need to put in great effort or hard work to finally accomplish the important goals of knowing yourself and creating self-love.

The Root Cause of Self-Loathing

Our thought processes are like little entities that permeate our mind and pass through it with thousands of thoughts per day, going over and over about what we have done, all we have experienced, stories involving others and ourselves. It is a relationship with ourselves that sometimes we like and sometimes we loathe.

From this ongoing relationship with the mind of unwanted thoughts, it is important to remember that thinking about something that has happened, whether a few minutes ago or a decade ago, is no longer relevant because life only exists in the narrow gate of each present moment. Spending time going over the events that occurred the same day, yesterday or even decades ago is useless!

Through our imagination, we may relive an event and the people who took part in that event from our past. And our physical body feels it as if it is happening now!

Much of what we imagine, think, and believe is negative, often distorting the truth of what was said, and what really happened. It is usually done unconsciously. However, as we go over and over the same memory, we believe the memory that we have made up, and it becomes very real to us.

Worse yet, when we think of a past negative memory that causes an overwhelming emotion, we are re-living it in that moment, as if it is happening all over again, affecting us mentally, emotionally, and even physically. These thoughts produce an unfavorable mental image, affecting how we see ourselves. It is estimated that about sixty thousand mostly negative thoughts pass through our mind every day. All negative thoughts re-enforce the person that is not who we are. We are in essence living with an entity that constantly criticizes, complains, and lashes out, demoralizing our spirit. Don't believe the one who takes over and judges you. Can this be the cause of low self-esteem, self-hatred and self-loathing?

You Are Fine Just the Way You Are. You Are Simply Removing the Person You Are Not

Remember that letting go of the image we see in the mirror leads to an understanding of who we really are. Our life changes when we understand we are a spiritual being having a human existence. There is a depth within each of us that goes far beyond the small mind of continual negative chatter. The spiritual depth is what we all seek at some point in our life and has always been there awaiting our recognition. The outer shell we see daily in the mirror because it changes and transforms as we age, may produce judgment and criticism toward ourselves. The true essence of vibrancy and spark within the human spirit as we age is completely overlooked. Everything changes when we recognize who we are and realize our connection to an eternal Universal Source energy. You are little by little recognizing who you are as you practice here.

As you know yourself as a Divine connection to something Greater, there is no judgment, no opinion, nor assessment of yourself. You simply are. And you accept yourself as you are.

Dissolving Bothersome Thoughts

The way to alleviate and dissolve negative thoughts that cause self-loathing, and low self-esteem is by noticing the patterns of thoughts that are a cause of suffering. This is done by going beyond the mind toward the positive thoughts of a higher consciousness, which you are accomplishing as you do the meditative practices here. Remember that going beyond the mind is the spiritual practice of ascending to the higher mind of higher consciousness. This is the path you are already on as you practice here. As you make space between your thoughts through practicing mindful meditation that is part of your journey of ascension, it will be easier to notice the patterns of thoughts that cause suffering and hardship.

Of course, ascending higher consciousness does not happen overnight. There will be moments when the energy of unwanted thoughts is still infiltrating the mind.

However, as you develop the *Presence of higher consciousness* you are gaining qualities of discernment, sensitivity, and compassion. If an unloving thought comes through about someone or something, you can now acknowledge the thought with compassionate, kind firmness. Say, "That is not true," and follow with a more elevated thought about the situation or person. You are not fighting the thought, so that the mind of unwanted thoughts simply subsides and does not fight back.

Remember that unloving thoughts about others are a reflection of our own thoughts about ourselves. When we are critical and judgmental of others, we are critical and judgmental of ourselves!

When we absorb daily fear from headlines and news, it entrenches in our mind and body, affecting our health. And it does not stop there because living with fear is detrimental to every corner of our life. Fear affects our perspective of life, our very outlook about the way we look at life, and the quality of our relationships. The low energy of fear turns into cynicism, distrust, and contempt. The fearful contempt we feel can in turn lead to self-loathing. As we continue feeling fear, we resist it by fighting it. But that only blocks the good and pure qualities of the higher consciousness we deserve. Remember that what we resist persists.

Focus on Your Strengths!

As your mind becomes more spacious, you can create purposeful, deliberate affirmed thoughts about yourself. Begin by considering your strengths. What are your talents? What do you love to do?

You may believe you do not have talent. A talent usually revolves around something you love to do. We all have something we enjoy doing that leads to a fulfilling, enjoyable life. The truth is you are a genuinely important and powerful person, able to create the kind of life you want. You are a drop in the ocean of life with the power of the ocean!

This power awakens when you recognize the truth and begin living in Presence. Presence will be discussed more fully in a later chapter.

As you become positive, and you will as you consistently practice here, thoughts about yourself will slowly but surely help you develop self-love. The negative thoughts that once ruled your life will simply fall by the wayside. As you commit and have an intention to continue practicing here, there is no doubt you will see an improvement in weeks and months in all aspects of your life.

The ease, relaxation, and peace that will help you ascend into higher consciousness and finally reveal your true self and true nature is simple. However, keep in mind that letting go of the entity-like thoughts that are so distracting will take patience and a real commitment to remember to stay on the path toward a better, more fulfilling life. That part may not be easy.

Our world is filled with a path full of potholes of things not going right! Remember to observe from a distance the thoughts and emotions that cause stress, anxiety, anger, hopelessness, fear or any conflict so that you do not pollute your inner being. Because if we allow negativity to infiltrate our mind repeatedly, we will always be blocked and hindered from the experience of loving who we really are.

Challenge Negative Thoughts About Yourself!

As you go about your day, if you experience the chatter of the small mind putting out negative thoughts, always challenge these unwanted thoughts. Remember to say, "That's not true!" and replace it with a positive thought that is the opposite of the unwelcome, unwanted thought. It could be an affirmation you verbalize daily or anything that reveals your newfound good feelings and thoughts about yourself. If a thought comes through the ordinary mind telling you "Nobody likes me!" it could be turned into, "That's not true, I am likeable because I always look for the best in people."

Practice Self-Compassion

As you practice and meditate in this book, you are learning unconditional love, non-judgment, loving kindness, appreciation, gratitude, and many higher ways of being. You are gaining qualities that are naturally directed toward the Self, creating self-love and self-esteem.

Have compassion for the self that has brought you to this point. The self that did the best you knew how in difficult circumstances. You are now on a journey that is releasing the self that continually suffered through listening to the negative thoughts coming from the small, false ego self. And you are doing it kindly and gently as you practice peaceful relaxation.

Anything learned in peaceful relaxation is something that will endure. Each time you practice mindfulness, you are focusing on your breath, and as you notice a thought, you are training your mind to come back again and again to your breath in the present moment. Much more is happening than you know! You are loving yourself through patience and compassion. And you are also present in the moment, creating a spacious mind that is calmer and less affected by negativity.

Be Kind to Yourself

Remember that as you are present, you are not criticizing, condemning, nor complaining about anything, anyone, or yourself. So that as you practice being present here you are also practicing self-love. More will be discussed about the present moment in a later chapter. In fact, all the practices you are doing here help you to be present in the moment and with compassionate kindness toward yourself. And this happens the same moment you let go of stress, anger, or fear and shift to feeling peaceful, calm, and re-laxed.

Keep in mind that as you practice calming peace, neg-ative words like fear, anger, or stress are no longer a part of who you are. You are gaining strength, stabil-ity, dependability, reliability, composure, and calm-ness. These are only a few powerfully descriptive words that you gain as you ascend higher conscious-ness.

Meditative Practice J

Gaining Strength and Stability As You Ground Yourself

In the following practice feel the strength and stabil-ity of grounding yourself:

Take a few comfortable breaths until you feel at peace. Inhale slightly longer than you normally do. And as you exhale, with your feet firmly on the ground, imagine you have roots that go deep all the way to the core and heart center of Mother Earth. As you inhale imagine you are bringing Mother Earth's energy up into your solar plexus, near your navel. Pause there for a couple of seconds, then lift your energy up to your heart, and up to your mind. As you exhale, bring your energy down again to the core of Mother Earth. And, as you inhale, bring the energy up again to your solar plexus, heart, and mind. Imagine the energy in the form of a triangle and continue for as long as you like.

You are safe and secure, and gaining strength and stability.

Energy from the Earth's core strengthens self-esteem as you find the heart and core of Mother Earth that nurtures, heals, and loves unconditionally. Practicing being grounded helps to maintain a sense of detachment in a more *feeling* state.

You are learning a more feeling state in which you no longer avoid or suppress emotions. Your thoughts and feelings are now linked to the higher mind of a higher consciousness in which speaking your truth becomes smoother, flowing, and effortless.

Every moment you spend setting aside time for self-care practices like meditation, connecting with nature, and being present now is a moment that is monumental on your path toward higher consciousness, which includes feeling the freedom of letting go.

Respect the time that you spend with yourself. As you practice here and meditate, immerse yourself in the moment that you spend within. There is nothing you must do in those moments, nowhere you must be. It is an important time to set aside just for you because you are giving benefit to every corner of your life as you do!

Have Self-Compassion as You May Still Overthink the Problems of a Difficult World

There are times when you may still overthink the problems, situations, and everything that goes on in an unstable, concerning world.

There is no doubt we live in a difficult world that is constantly changing, depriving us of a grounded, reliable stability. You may, at times, still try to find a resolution through overthinking about problems, situations, and everything that goes on in a problematic world. However, as you now know, solving problems through the small mind never works. As a result, we are more anxious, worried, and unsettled than ever, affecting our health and well-being.

Meditative Practice K

Love-Giving Powers to Relieve Overthinking

If you want calmer, more peaceful emotions, if your mind is overworked from overthinking and you'd like to soothe it, the angel realm can help you through the energy of love they emit. In the following practice you are offered love and soothing

restoration for your emotional, mental, and physical bodies:

Take three or four relaxing, calming breaths or as many as you need to feel at peace. Once you are at peace, teleport to the realm where angels offer love-giving powers. They know you are coming, and a group of angels welcomes you. Feel the vibrational energy of love they emit. You can feel their love and care just by being in their presence. An angel steps forward to ask if you would like their transmission of soothing, restorative love so that you can 'change your life for the better.' Let them know you want this energy of love. They form a circle around you, each angel amplifying the vibrational energy of love to repair your emotional and mental bodies so that your physical body is more balanced and har-monized, restoring its perfect patterns.

Allow the energy they transmit to reach your cellu-lar level. All areas that need transformation are be-ing tapped by the vibrational energy of love that the angels emit. Troubling thoughts coming from an overworked, overthinking mind is now soothed.

You are feeling calm, rested, and more at peace. Feel the energy of love the angels are infusing throughout your mental and emotional bodies. They want you to know that you can tap into their vibrational energy as you think of them because they are always available.

Thank them for their love, care, and compassion, as you teleport back from where you started.

You have done more than you know as you do this meditative practice. You are not only increasing self-love, but you are benefiting your health and well-being, leading you to a more fulfilled and happier life.

Overthinking Robs You of the Peace You Deserve

Remember that when you are worried about someone or something, you are overthinking a thought again and again with no resolution, robbing you of peace, joy, and enthusiasm for life. Uncontrolled, it can destroy health causing a spectrum of diseases. When we are not at ease, the human physical body is not "in the flow" working on our behalf, without interference, in the perfect way it was meant to work.

When we overthink a relationship, we create inaccurate narratives such as "I'm not getting enough attention, maybe he/she wants to break up," or imagine worst-case scenarios like "I can see them leaving." We begin to believe what we are thinking and imagining.

This kind of rumination leads to low feelings of self-worth and self-esteem especially if negative overthinking results in a failed relationship. And of course, keep in mind that if we continue to harbor negativity within a relationship, it is bound to fail.

It's important to remember that these thoughts, emotions, ruminations, and imaginings that do not make us feel good are false, because they come from the small, false mind.

The reason this mind is false is because you have the power within you to rise above and go beyond the small mind that causes harm and hardship. You have every tool within you, and you have it now, at this moment. You can quiet the thoughts and shift the emotions toward a better life experience.

CHAPTER SIX:

OPENING THE HEART TO LOVE

"To love is to recognize yourself in another" –
Eckart Tolle

Love is the answer. It is love that heals all fear, all negativity. Love is the fundamental energy in the Universe of purity and goodness that encompasses all worlds. In the same way that fear in our third-dimensional Earth life is the underlying cause of emotions that hinder and block us, its contrast is love, which opens the path to a fulfilling and happy life.

Love does not judge, and has no doubt, worry, or anger. The path you are on of higher consciousness, like love, is indescribable. There are no words that can describe the feelings of unconditional love, peace, joy, and bliss.

Love does not need thought. It cannot be refuted, contested, or negated. Its strength and foundation rests in the awareness of those we love. And that is enough because there is nothing more that is needed in the warm glow of loving appreciation for another.

Consider for a moment about how you feel about your loved ones, your friends, partners, pets, and life itself. There are simply no words that can come close to conveying the beautiful feeling of love.

Meditative Practice L

Being Light and Love to Overcome Fearful Thoughts

Love coming from Source energy, of which we are a part, is obscured when we feel fear. Imagine our physical sun being obscured by passing clouds, allowing only a trickle of sunlight to come through. Imagine that you are the sunlight, which is life, light, and love itself! The love that you are is being obscured by the passing, fleeting clouds of thoughts and emotions!

In the following practice, use your imagination and feel peaceful tranquility when you are fearful about

a worrisome situation. Calm your emotions and feel secure and at peace.

Take a few deep, comfortable, relaxing breaths. Imagine you are the sun's brilliant light. You are life itself and love itself as you radiate light to all life. Notice the passing clouds of worrisome situations and see them dissolved as your light becomes stronger, nourishing and benefiting life. Immerse and saturate yourself in this light, letting it permeate through your whole body. Feel the peaceful, serene energy of love that cannot be destroyed.

Remember you are Source energy, and you have the source energy of love within. You are cultivating and amplifying it here with intention. Love is the highest energy and promotes a soothing effect, overcoming the anxiety and stress of fear.

You are doing much more than you know as you amplify the love that is already a part of you. You are letting go and surrendering when you feel the energy of love.

You may receive love from someone that supports

you, calming your concerns and worries. You may experience oxytocin, a feel-good hormone that your body produces when you are loved.

However, you are also promoting many health benefits when you experience the love you are radiating toward situations and others. New neuropathways are being created as you practice an expansion of the energy of love within you. The new neuropathways of an amplification of love within are beneficial to health and well-being.

Imagine neuropathways in your brain like highways and roads that are being used again and again. If you have a worrisome thought that you think hundreds of times daily, it becomes like a trench that is so deep the mind is stuck in it, producing stress, insecurity, anxiety, and fear. So that as you practice a new pathway, the mind will leave the old pathway and create a new neuropathway in your brain. As you ascend into higher consciousness, you are creating new neuropathways in your brain and a more positive high energy of love is being developed that is better for your health and well-being, and your entire life!

Opening Your Heart Allows a Better Relationship With Others and Yourself

There is nothing but good that comes from the activation of heart-felt, loving, and kind feelings that the heart is capable of projecting, changing every corner of your life.

The energy around our heart is vibrant and alive, already equipped, organized, and primed for complete activation within you. It is your center, a fundamental piece of the puzzle of who you are.

Going back millennia in history, humans have known that the heart is the center, core, and focal point within each of us. Derived from the word core, the word Corazón in Spanish and Portuguese means heart. Your heart is your core and essence, like the nucleus of an atom.

And like the nucleus of an atom, the heart is a crucial center that integrates the superb engineering of your physical body, influencing and affecting the way it behaves.

Imagine feeling free because you have let go of thoughts and emotions that once caused you pain and suffering. You no longer feel pushed down and weighted. There is lightness in your heart, in your whole being. Moreover, it is felt by others, consciously or unconsciously, because just as a smile is contagious, so is the feeling of a magnetic heart.

Love transcends everything. Love is the highest, most powerful energy in the universe. In the same way, it is fundamental, primary, and centralized within us. It carries the energy of the Universal Energy of Love.

Meditative Practice M

Merging with the Universal Energy of Love

Love is the primary energy within all life forms everywhere and all around us.

In the following practice, you are practicing going into the energy of Universal Love:

Take a few comfortable breaths until you feel

peaceful, calm tranquility. Imagine a slightly up-hill, spiral path in front of you surrounded by a beautiful meadow filled with blooming flowers of all colors. Everything you see is perfect.

The sky is a deep blue, and the sunlight is coming in through the top of your head, flooding you with a warm, peaceful feeling from the top of your head to your toes. The higher you go the more beautiful are the vistas around you. The colors are more vibrant than you've ever seen before.

In the distance, you hear the soft sound of a heartbeat beckoning you to come closer. It is the heartbeat and center of Universal Love. The heartbeat becomes louder, and the closer you come to it, the more magnetic you are to it. As you arrive at its center, you feel a deep inner peace. Your heartbeat matches the Universal heartbeat of love coming from Source Energy. You are regenerated as you inhale, and love is expanded as you exhale good and pure energy of love out to the world. The unwanted energies you have picked up through life are dissolved because they cannot survive in the elevated energy of Universal Love. Stay here as long as you like and come as often as you like.

As you do this practice, you are in the still, silent place of your true nature and true identity. Every moment spent here is a moment that frees you and allows you to let go. You feel blissfully peaceful. You have stopped the noisy mind of its continual chatter, now silenced because you are at peace in the high vibrational frequency of love.

As you continue and commit to this practice you will begin to feel the interconnectedness of all life, to know who you really are, to grow in the feeling of unconditional love, and to feel, little by little, the movement of vibration and frequency.

Flourishing Relationships

Relationships flourish into loving relationships when we intuitively know and feel the essence of the other person. As we expand our consciousness, we join our friends and loved ones in voicing our opinion, because as we let go and feel free the stage is set to detach from needing an outcome to be a certain way. Acceptance is an important part of not trying to change anyone's point of view. Our point of view does not come from a need to be right but from a place that is stable and secure without a need to persuade or sway opinions.

The higher state of consciousness we experience allows us to be aware of others. With increased intuition we know when it is appropriate to speak honestly about our point of view or when we should just listen. Higher consciousness allows us to have clarity and honesty in thought and to disallow being confrontational. Our committed practice of observation allows us to accept all points of view, to simply be, without trying to change another person's viewpoint.

When We Fall in Love, Are We in Control?

When the ego mind "falls" in love, there is an attraction of the shell of the person, the "shallow," and not the true spirit and heart. When we fall in love it may be the way someone looks, acts, and speaks.

However, each person continually changes, so that the way we look, speak, and act alters and transforms. The question that remains is whether love will endure.

Remember that we are not the physical self we see in the mirror. The physical body is continually changing through the years and decades. If the unconscious mind falls in love with the looks and personality of the ever-changing self, would "love" still be there as the shell of the physical body transforms and gradually ages?

It does not mean that the love that emerges from physical attraction cannot survive. It can survive with an element of knowing the *true essence* present in the other person, which is already within each of us.

Once the romantic and infatuated aspect of the relationship comes to an end, as it always does, a more stable quality comes to the surface which can potentially make both parties satisfied and happy in the relationship.

As we grow in higher consciousness, the small mind dissolves making way for the higher mind of wisdom and discernment. And as we integrate higher consciousness into daily life, it leads to qualities of integrity and wisdom, which is what truly matters in life. As we transcend and go beyond the small mind we now know and feel the true essence and spirit of a person. That's when true love emerges and is felt.

Transcending and going beyond the everyday mind is finding the true nature of our true self. We no longer indulge in the low energies of the hysterical and fear-driven thoughts of the small mind.

Instead, we have committed an intention to immerse and saturate our mind with only positive "vibes," taking us to the highest energies of vibration and frequency. Staying within this energy is what helps to bring about the life we've always wanted because the energy of a high vibrational frequency attracts the same kind of good energy into our life. Now there is no need to seek love because love always finds us. We have merged with the eternal, stable Universal Energy of Love.

Universal Source Energy Gives Back When We Appreciate

The energy we receive from cultivating and expressing appreciation and gratitude is loving and boundless. It is a gift from Universal Source that keeps on giving. I have already discussed appreciation and gratitude in a prior chapter as well as in prior books. In this chapter, we will explore more of the infinite energy available as you appreciate and have gratitude in daily life.

More on the Difference Between Appreciation and Gratitude

According to Esther Hicks, author and spiritual leader, gratitude involves a transition from something that we experienced in hardship and suffering to a relief of that suffering. Gratitude is more temporary than appreciation. Let's say someone had an automobile accident and has now recovered their health and their car. They are grateful. And let's say someone has recovered from a serious illness. They are grateful. A subtle thought of a negative transition may prevent the whole and complete expansion of appreciation.

Appreciation is being aware of the flow all around us that makes life possible. The sun and the rain that heal, regenerate, and replenish life. The amazing engineering of our physical body, and its perfect function without our need to control its systems.

While having gratitude is powerful, appreciation is expansive because there is no end to what we can and should appreciate! And it can be done a hundred times a day, greatly elevating and easily maintaining our vibration and frequency moment by moment.

Is an Understanding of What Life Truly Offers Us Being Neglected and Not Taught?

We teach our children to be grateful by saying "thank you," which may come about remotely without a true understanding of what it means to be grateful. Is it only about receiving material gifts?

Appreciation can be fostered and nurtured in every moment of our lives. As we appreciate everything we see, smell, hear, taste, and touch—even the smallest things—we develop a good habit that grows in our experience. The habit of appreciation opens our heart, creates self-love, and simply makes life easier with less struggle. We are focusing on an elevated energy affecting us physically, mentally, and emotionally in a good and healthy way. As we develop the positive habit of appreciation, our mind, our outlook on life, and our attitude can actually change our life for the better in just weeks.

Our relationships improve because people like to be around positive, good-natured people. We are up-lifted and can feel, consciously or unconsciously, the higher energy that an appreciative person of a higher consciousness radiates.

Because of our committed and intentioned habit of appreciation, our health and well-being improve when we no longer foster negativity that contributes to ill health.

Appreciating everything opens our heart. With an open heart

we radiate the Universal Energy of Love, a powerful energy attracting the life we've always wanted.

When we focus on appreciating life, moment by moment, the energy of love is expressed. With a focused mind on only the positive and appreciative aspects of life, there is no doubt our life gets better and better.

Meditative Practice N

The Angel Realm Offers Comforting Powers

There is no doubt the world we live in is more distracting than it has ever been. Instantly, we know what is happening all over the world.

Even though you now have the tools to turn away from disturbing situations, it is natural for the distracting world at large to bleed through the calming peace you have cultivated and now express. As a result, anxious, unsettling worry may still be affecting your health and well-being.

If you need reassurance or encouragement. If you

are experiencing a situation that is too heavy to bear, or have pain in your heart, open yourself to the following meditative practice:

Take several comfortable, relaxing breaths until you feel peaceful. You are teleporting once again to the realm where angels know you are coming and welcome you with open arms. You feel the loving comfort they emit. A group gathers around you in a circle, offering you the energy of loving comfort. Each amplifies the highest energy of love to soothe any pain in your heart, anything that has made you feel alone and isolated. You feel at peace, calm, and relaxed. Through the energy of love they emit, you feel more whole, complete, and stronger. Their soothing, comforting love has restored you. You may stay as long as you like. They want you to know you can come to them for comfort any time you think of them because they are always available.

Thank them for their care and love as you come back into the space where you began your journey.

You have done more than you know as you do this meditative practice. You are not only opening your heart, but you are benefiting your health and well-being, as you release any burden leading you to a more fulfilled and happier life.

CHAPTER SEVEN:

LIVING IN THE PRESENT

MOMENT

The past has no power over the present moment-
Eckhart Tolle

Living present, moment by moment, is not the end of the journey to higher consciousness. It is the start of a mysteriously beautiful beginning. It is an opening of every fiber of your being — your heart, your soul, and a mind that has transcended and gone beyond the limited everyday mind that once caused havoc in life.

Moment by moment, present awareness changes your life. Powerful energies begin to work on your behalf. It is as if because you have let go and freed yourself of the limiting nature of the small mind, you are rewarded with the kind of life you have always wanted and richly deserve.

Can you be aware with a keen focus of your sight, hearing, smell, taste, and touch?

Yes, of course, each of us can be aware and fully focused on our senses.

As you look around at what surrounds you, can you simply look without naming or labelling what you see? Can you take in the essence and not the label or scientific name of a flower?

According to spiritual leader and author, Eckart Tolle, our tendency is to conceptualize everything we see, without allowing the natural intelligence within us to come to the surface.

Thoughts come to the surface that produce suppositions, theories, or guesses. As we look at flowers we may verbalize or think, "This one is not as pretty as the one over there," or "What year was it when I took that trip and saw a flower exactly like this one?"

We completely miss the freedom and letting go that

we are given in the present moment — feeling replenished and restored in the enjoyment and pleasure of a simple moment.

As you look around, can you merge with focus on your senses and at the same time on your inner being, the still place within?

As you gain higher consciousness, and merge with the feeling of your inner being and simultaneously focus on your senses, the thinking everyday mind pauses in quietude and silence.

It might take a little practice, however, as you create space between your thoughts, it will become easier.

The practice, then, is to let go of the thoughts that take you away from the present moment. Mindfulness will help you practice present-moment awareness by focusing on your breath and coming back again and again to your breath when you become aware of an unwanted thought. This is a good way to learn to focus on the present moment without allowing the perilous thinking of unwanted thoughts to come to the surface. As you are fully present in non-thought, you are in the rich and powerful core of yourself attracting miraculous events into life that will begin making their appearance in weeks or months.

Unwanted thoughts that cause suffering and block pleasure, enjoyment, and peace in the *now* moment hold you either in the past where there is sadness, anger, and despair or in the future where there is worry and stress.

Remember that neither the past nor the future are relevant or important because the only place life truly exists is now, in this moment.

All Valuable Action Is in the Present Moment

The most important action you can take is to *feel calming peace and joy in this moment.* The next highest order of action needed is "working" on your goal in the moment. Something we love to do is not considered work. You may have already noticed how "time flies" when you are doing something you love. When we have a goal in mind, remember that we cannot control the outcome of a goal because there are many moving parts in the outer world that influence the goal. However, we *do* have the awareness to create our best work now, improving the successful trajectory and outcome of a goal.

All too often our focus is on the result when pursuing a goal. We are not enjoying the journey of the goal which is the present moment. Instead, we are anticipating and yearning for the "happiness" that the result will give us. We are missing every moment of the journey, which is the real and true prize.

Remember that the power comes not from yearning nor the eager anticipation of what we want in the future, but from our aware *Presence* in this moment, now.

Often, we experience an attachment to the result, which is the thoughtform of the everyday mind believing the destination we yearn for is most important. We are detached when we are in the peaceful joy of the moment, fully enjoying the journey. The trick then is not to become attached to its outcome but detached as you work with attentive care and awareness in the present moment. You are learning to detach as you are practicing and meditating in this book.

The True Goal Is Presence Now

Any activity requires *alert awareness* and the more you practice presence, the more you will experience the clarity and keen awareness that doing good work requires. This is how you will experience a successful result of your goal.

If we are not living life now, in this moment, we are not living life. We are missing each slice of the moments of our life!

Being peaceful and joyful in the moment is the most important goal. From that point everything becomes easier and more effortless.

In my life, when I become aware that my mind is producing memories of the past—thoughts of people, thoughts of things and situations—I immediately pause and shift my thinking to more elevated thoughts concerning people, things, and situations. I realize more than ever that thoughts of this kind are useless and hinder and block my expansion and growth into higher consciousness which benefits not only myself but everyone around me.

Being and having Presence is an expansion of aware-ness and of higher consciousness. Remember that awareness *is* consciousness, the higher consciousness we are ascending. And as we expand and evolve, just as the infinite Universe that we are a part of expands, more beautiful gifts and rewards await.

As we listen and allow thoughts to come through the noisy mind that continually has us thinking of the past, we believe that our identification of who we are is what we experienced in the past. If we continue to believe that is who we are, we will continue to suffer the hardship of thoughts and emotions coming from the small self.

We engage in fear as we identify with our form and the forms of everything around us. There is a time el-ement when it comes to form in our third dimensional world. There is a beginning and an end to every form, whether a material object or a person. Everything that we experience comes to an end: a career, a relationship, an inanimate object that weathers and corrodes with age.

However, as we shift our attention, focus, and awareness to the present moment we let go of feeling fear. The present moment is timeless. It is just here, right now. We now know that we too are timeless, everlasting, infinite beings. We lose the fear of sadness, anger, resentment, unforgiveness, regret, future worry, tension, stress, and anxiety. And we lose fear, also, of the inevitable end of our earthly existence.

You are an infinite being whose life does not end with this physical existence. You are a Universal Source energy that is immortal and eternal!

What Blocks Us From Being Present

We may believe that being present moment by moment may sound too simple. Can it be that simple to fix depressed, disheartened, and desperate issues in life?

It *is* simple to live in the present moment, however, it is not easy to commit and have daily intention to practice presence because we, as a society, are so distracted by the experiences we have daily. The agitations and disruptions of daily life are complicated, complex, and extremely difficult.

The present moment is the prize of a higher consciousness. The answer to feeling free and letting go is your aware *Presence* in this moment. In the same moment you are present, you have already let go. And you are already free.

Feel the tranquility and the peace when you are *Present* and aware. In presence, the mind of unwanted thoughts softens, becoming silent.

A Simple Way to Raise Your Mood

Spiritual leader and author Eckart Tolle tells us that the first thing to do when we want to raise our mood, our vibration and frequency is to look around at our surroundings. This puts us in the present moment, aware and focused on the now moment. Remember that awareness and focus are powerful tools you can use to shift a mood into a higher vibration within you.

If you want to take this step further, look at the details of the room you are in or the outside you are at. Notice what perhaps you have never noticed before. If you normally sit facing a certain wall in the room, go to another side of the room and see it from another perspective. Look at every detail. Or if outside, notice the trees and the plants that perhaps you have never noticed before. Notice every detail. You might think of this as "stopping to smell the roses," something we have lost sight of in our rushed society. Breath in the air and think of relaxation and peace. Commune with nature because it regenerates and revitalizes us emotionally and mentally.

You may be thinking that you don't have time to do this because you have too much to do. You do not have the time *not* to do it!

Remember that when you are present and aware,

even for seconds in your day, you are doing much more than you realize. In the same moment you have presence, you are relieving your mind and body of dis-ease. You have found calming peace and are creating space in between your thoughts. Your mind has quieted, opening your ability to receive wise intuitive guidance. Your elevated energy now attracts the same good and pure energy through better, more elevated situations and circumstances in your life. Most important, you are living your life in the only place life truly exists. Gone are the ruminating, unwanted thoughts and emotions of the past, where life no longer exists. Your life is moving forward because you now have the space to create the life you want.

Observing Without Thoughts

As you look around at your surroundings in focused, alert awareness, use your sense of sight to really see a nature scene or the contents of a room without thought. The analytical mind may want to come in to count, measure, describe, identify, or classify. However, once you have a focused awareness without the clutter of thought, you are "consciousness at rest," a powerful place to *be*. You may simply put alert awareness on any sound you hear, either the chirping of birds or the hum of an air conditioner, without thought, and without a need to classify or describe. Remember that alert awareness is the key to a transformed life.

The forms that distract us in daily life, the homes, cars, TVs, computers, phones or the items in a room like tables and chairs are given much importance in life.

Yet, we completely miss what is the most important. The spaciousness that surrounds all the forms in our lives.

As we become more aware, we begin to naturally take in the spaciousness of a room or a nature scene. The space, the air that allows us to breathe, without which our life could not be possible!

Consider for a moment the significance of the space in a room or outdoors. Is the air and space not the most important of all?

Remember each of us is the spaciousness within. It is what you give focus, attention, and awareness when you meditate and when you practice in this book.

The inner space within is most important because as we put awareness on our inner spaciousness, we change our life for the better. Remember that awareness of our spaciousness within is *Presence*. In presence, we have let go and we are free of all that once caused great upheaval in our lives.

Remember, as you merge the spaciousness of a room or the outdoors with your inner space, you have Presence.

There is no duality, no opposition, when you merge the spaciousness of your inner being with the outer world. There is only one.

As you continue putting awareness on yourself within, your *feeling* state, notice that the noisy mind has softened, becoming quieter.

In presence, you are in resonance with Universal

Source energy — the Divine — and you are powerful!

In *Presence,* you are self-aware and one with all life.

The present moment is a powerful place to **be.**

As you experience the outer world daily, *Presence* will help you to recognize when something feels draining and unaligned with your energy and values.

Presence cannot be disrupted or disturbed. It is indestructible and immeasurable. It is The All that Is and Universal Source energy.

As you practice the path of higher consciousness here you are little by little becoming *Presence!* And it all has to do with awareness of the rich space, the treasure trove, within the center of yourself.

I invite you to continue the peaceful calm you have experienced here. Because there are many more gifts and rewards in store for you as you continue this journey.

Feel the Feeling of Letting Go

You now can feel what it feels like to let go. There is

one more feeling that is the goal of letting go — feeling free.

In freedom we have cast away burdens. We feel lighter in spirit and in our physical body. We no longer carry the heavy baggage of anger, guilt, regret, resentment, stress, anxiety, fear, tension. Nor do we carry the heavy load of envy, jealousy, disillusionment, hate, malice, rage, revenge, or hopelessness. I may have missed a multitude of many other words that make up the emotions that we as human collectives know so well.

What a burden it has been! What a waste of precious life!

It is so simple and uncomplicated to be free! When you are free, you simply *feel* peace, joy, and vibrant aliveness.

You can now feel the genuine, Greater, best version of yourself. The more peaceful, joyous, and more vibrantly alive *You*.

EASY ACCESS

TO MEDITATIVE PRACTICES

∞

Meditative Practice A: Reaching Your Peaceful Center

In the following meditation, you are reaching the core of yourself where there is peace as you become free and let go:

Inhale comfortably through your nose with your mouth closed. As you exhale, part your lips slightly and breathe out all tension and stress. Continue inhaling and exhaling in the same way releasing tension and stress more and more. Tense your feet for three to four seconds then release and feel relaxation in your feet. Continue tensing for three to four seconds, and releasing your legs, thighs, torso, shoulders, and neck in the same way. Relax the muscles in your face and around your eyes, allowing your mouth to drop slightly. Put attention and focus on your breath and the peaceful calm of your body. Stay here as long as you like.

So much more is happening here than you realize. You are relieving your mental, emotional, and physical body, which leads to better health and well-being. You are present, aware... you have let go, and you are free. When you have Presence, you are living your life in the only place life truly exists, now, in this moment! When your mind is in the past or the future in worry, you are simply not living life!

Meditative Practice B: Letting Go of Stress

The following meditation will give you the feeling of lightness, easing your stress. It can be done quickly by taking just a moment from your day:

Sit in a comfortable position as you inhale through your nose. Exhale as if through a straw, imagining you are letting go of all stress that is turning into a brilliant light in front of you. Continue inhaling and exhaling in the same way until you let go, feel calm, at peace, and free of stress. Maintain the feeling of calming peace for as long as you like.

This practice helps you to let go and feel free. As you imagine stress turning into light, you are not fighting the energy of stress but allowing it to dissolve in a kind and loving way. Keep in mind that resisting any thought or emotion of a lower energy through fighting and battling never works because it will come back with a vengeance!

Meditative Practice C: Relieving Emotional Stress

When you experience a sudden stressful emotion coming from a sensory perception that triggers a memory of a stressful event, take a moment to pause.

Take a deeper breath than you normally do and inhale with your mouth closed. Then exhale with your mouth slightly open. Continue inhaling and exhaling in the same way until you are relaxed, at peace, and free of stress.

Dissolving stress can be done effortlessly as you take comfortable, relaxing breaths.

In an instant, the mind can take you on a chain of unwanted thoughts that keeps you stuck in emotional stress.

As you continue the practice of relaxation and peace the breath creates, the mind and body will sooner than later adapt to your new way of being.

Meditative Practice D: Becoming Familiar With Your True Identity

As we practice meditation, or what is referred to as mindfulness, we are practicing becoming familiar with our inner being, the space within ourselves, our identity and true nature. This is the space within us that through cultivation, nurturing, and finally expressing it, moment by moment, is what leads to letting go and freeing us so that we can live a happier, more rewarding life.

In the following practice, you are becoming *familiar* with your inner self, who you really are, your true self and true nature.

Take a few relaxing breaths until you feel calm, relaxed, and at peace. Put *aware* focus on your breath. As you take a few focused, relaxing breaths, notice the mind quiets down when you are aware and focused. If your mind wanders, bring it back again and again to an aware focus on your breath. Continue until you feel completely relaxed and at peace.

As you practice a meditative state of awareness and focus on your inner self and breath, you have let go of anger, hopelessness, sadness, regret, fear, tension, and stress.

You may do this mindfulness meditative practice daily for five to ten minutes as you begin, increasing the practice to fifteen minutes or more as you become more and more familiar and comfortable with the spaciousness within you.

Meditative Practice E: Softening and Quieting the Mind

Keep in mind that even as you practice awareness and meditation, you may become aware of unhelpful thoughts that trigger emotions like sadness, anger, anxiety, or stress. It does not mean that you are failing as you practice awareness. Awareness takes consistency and commitment. Accept the unhelpful thoughts without battle or fight, and simply continue a practice of a focused, relaxed, calm peace.

Relax as you inhale and exhale comfortably focusing on your breath so that your mind softens and quiets down. As you become aware of a thought coming through, say, "next thought please," and simply wait for the next thought. You will notice that the mind becomes unbelievably quiet!

If you have ever experienced hearing something in the middle of the night that awakens you, you become very alert and aware waiting for the next sound.

Meditative Practice F: Dissolving Overwhelming Emotions by Not Fighting Them

Remember that through embracing and accepting overwhelming emotions and allowing them to flow without fighting them is how we dissolve them. We can then more easily find our way to the rich center within.

In the following practice, as soon as you feel the emotional energy charge of an overwhelming emotion, allow the emotion to pass through you, feeling its intensity as it dissolves:

Take slightly deeper comfortable breaths, accepting and allowing only the energy of emotion (not the thought) no matter how intense. Feel the intensity of the emotion, no matter how strong, until the energy of the emotion subsides. Revel in the tranquil peace as you continue focusing on your slowed down, easy breaths.

Feeling and allowing the emotion to pass through you, as you just did, is accepting the emotion, not fighting it. You are learning to feel emotion rather than suppressing or repressing it. You are allowing, accepting, and embracing an unwanted emotion to pass through you, so that little by little the overwhelming emotion will get weaker, lose its momentum, and subside altogether, never to bother you again.

Meditative Practice G: Detaching as You Observe Overwhelming Thoughts

In the following practice, you are simply observing, not fighting, and, at the same time, you are disidentifying from an overwhelming thought and the emotion it produces.

As soon as you become aware of an overwhelming thought, imagine it in front of you and at least ten feet away. You have detached from the thought and its emotion, and you are aware and present as you simply observe the thought from a distance. Observe it for as long as you like, imagining the thought or emotion transforming into light. In this moment you too, have transformed. You are aware and present. Revel in the peace and the freedom you feel as you let go.

A lot more than you may realize is happening in the moment you simply observe a thought from a distance.

Keep in mind that as soon as you are calm, simply observing thoughts and their emotions, allowing them to come and go, you have let go and you are free.

Meditative Practice H: Feeling Safe and Secure by Slowing Down Your Breathing

Remember that all behavior makes sense even when you experience an "unhealthy" over attachment. The following breathing practice will calm you.

The following is yet another way to dissolve an overwhelming feeling. In this case, an overwhelming feeling of attachment.

Remember the calming effects of your breath.

Put *aware focus* on a slightly deeper inhalation than normal with your mouth closed. And, as you exhale, part your lips slightly and imagine you are slowly breathing out the unwanted emotions causing suffering. Continue until you feel completely at peace.

As you do this, your mind and body slow down, causing rampant emotions to slow, and relieving you as you let go of the emotions that are detrimental to your health and well-being. The slowing-down effect of taking deep slow breaths activates your internal mechanism of feeling safe and secure.

Our heart rate slows, and our reactionary impulse softens, giving us a safe place to open, to be vulnerable.

Meditative Practice I: Feeling Peaceful as You Observe and Detach

As an observer you are detached from emotions of attachment in an easy and effortless way. There is no fight or battle. You are in peaceful tranquility as the emotions of attachment dissolve.

Any form of attachment that makes us feel bad is something we must dissolve.

In the following practice you are in a state of pure relaxation and peace as you feel emotions coming through, softening and dissolving.

Take a deeper, comfortable breath and exhale unwanted emotions of attachment. Continue taking comfortable breaths and exhaling emotions of attachment until you feel safe, calm and secure. As

you continue, take comfortable breaths and at the same time, put awareness on your entire body from your head to your toes. As you feel safe and secure, and at peace, is there an uncomfortable feeling someplace in your body? If so, feel it and allow it to slowly dissolve. As you feel each emotion that is uncomfortable, stay with each one, until each subsides and dissolves.

Remember that as you feel safe and secure, you become open. Your heart opens to compassion and love, and you feel safe enough to be vulnerable. You can now speak your feelings openly and honestly and without fear.

Meditative Practice J: Gaining Strength and Stability

In the following practice feel the strength and stability of grounding yourself:

Take a few comfortable breaths until you feel at peace. Inhale slightly longer than you normally do. And as you exhale, with your feet firmly on the ground, imagine you have roots that go deep all the way to the core and heart center of Mother Earth. As you inhale imagine you are bringing Mother Earth's energy up into your solar plexus, near your navel. Pause there for a couple of seconds, then lift your energy up to your heart, and up to your mind. As you exhale, bring your energy down again to the core of Mother Earth. And, as you inhale, bring the energy up again to your solar plexus, heart, and mind. Imagine the energy in the form of a triangle and continue for as long as you like.

You are safe and secure, and gaining strength and stability.

Energy from the Earth's core strengthens self-esteem as you find the heart and core of Mother Earth that nurtures, heals, and loves unconditionally. Practicing being grounded helps to maintain a sense of detachment in a more *feeling* state.

Meditative Practice K: Love-Giving Powers to Relieve Overthinking

If you want calmer, more peaceful emotions, if your mind is overworked from overthinking and you'd like to soothe it, the angel realm can help you through the energy of love they emit. In the following practice you are offered love and soothing restoration for your emotional, mental, and physical bodies:

Take three or four relaxing, calming breaths or as many as you need to feel at peace. Once you are at peace, teleport to the realm where angels offer love-giving powers. They know you are coming, and a group of angels welcomes you. Feel the vibrational energy of love they emit. You can feel their love and care just by being in their presence. An angel steps forward to ask if you would like their transmission of soothing, restorative love so that you can 'change your life for the better.' Let them know you want this energy of love. They form a circle around you, each angel amplifying the vibrational energy of love to repair your emotional and mental bodies so that your physical body is more balanced and harmonized, restoring its perfect patterns.

Allow the energy they transmit to reach your cellular level. All areas that need transformation are being tapped by the vibrational energy of love that the angels emit. Troubling thoughts coming from an overworked, overthinking mind are now soothed.

You are feeling calm, rested, and more at peace. Feel the energy of love the angels are infusing throughout your mental and emotional bodies. They want you to know that you can tap into their vibrational energy as you think of them because they are always available.

Thank them for their love, care, and compassion, as you teleport back from where you started.

You have done more than you know as you do this meditative practice. You are not only increasing self-love, but you are benefiting your health and well-being, leading you to a more fulfilled and happier life.

Meditative Practice L: Being Light and Love to Overcome Fearful Thoughts

Love coming from Source energy, of which we are a part, is obscured when we feel fear. Imagine our physical sun being obscured by passing clouds, allowing only a trickle of sunlight to come through. Imagine that you are the sunlight, which is life, light, and love itself! The love, light, and life that you are is being obscured by the passing, fleeting clouds of thoughts and emotions!

In the following practice, use your imagination and feel peaceful tranquility when you are fearful about a worrisome situation. Calm your emotions and feel secure and at peace.

Take a few deep, comfortable, relaxing breaths. Imagine you are the sun's brilliant light. You are life, light, and love as you radiate light to all life. Notice the passing clouds of worrisome situations and see them dissolved as your light becomes stronger, nourishing and benefiting life. Immerse and saturate yourself in this light, letting it permeate through your whole body. Feel the peaceful, serene energy of love that is indestructible.

Remember you are Source energy, and you have the source energy of love within. You are cultivating and amplifying it here with intention. Love is the highest energy and promotes a soothing effect, overcoming the anxiety and stress of fear.

You are doing much more than you know as you amplify the love that is already a part of you. You are letting go and surrendering when you feel the energy of love.

Meditative Practice M: Merging With the Energy of Universal Love

Love is the primary energy within all life forms everywhere and all around us.

In the following practice, you are practicing going into the energy of Universal Love:

Take a few comfortable breaths until you feel peaceful, calm tranquility. Imagine a slightly uphill, spiral path in front of you surrounded by a beautiful meadow filled with blooming flowers of all colors. Everything you see is perfect.

The sky is a deep blue, and the sunlight is coming in through the top of your head, flooding you with a warm, peaceful feeling from the top of your head

to your toes. The higher you go the more beautiful are the vistas around you. The colors are more vibrant than you've ever seen before.

In the distance, you hear the soft sound of a heartbeat beckoning you to come closer. It is the heartbeat and center of Universal Love. The heartbeat becomes louder, and the closer you come to it, the more magnetic you are to it. As you arrive at its center, you feel a deep inner peace. Your heartbeat matches the Universal heartbeat of love coming from Source Energy. You are regenerated as you inhale, and love is expanded as you exhale good and pure energy of love out to the world. The unwanted energies you have picked up through life are dissolved because they cannot survive in the elevated energy of Universal Love. Stay here as long as you like and come as often as you like.

As you do this practice, you are in the still, silent place of your true nature and true identity. Every moment spent here is a moment that frees you and allows you to let go. You feel blissfully peaceful. You have stopped the noisy mind of its continual chatter, now silenced because you are at peace in the high vibrational frequency of love.

Meditative Practice N: The Angel Realm Offers Comforting Powers

Even though you now have the tools to turn away from disturbing situations, it is natural for the distracting world at large to bleed through the calming peace you have cultivated and now express. As a result, anxious, unsettling worry may still be affecting your health and well-being.

If you need reassurance or encouragement. If you are experiencing a situation that is too heavy to bear, or have pain in your heart, open yourself to the following meditative practice:

Take several comfortable, relaxing breaths until you feel peaceful. You are teleporting once again to the realm where angels know you are coming and welcome you with open arms. You feel the loving comfort they emit. A group gathers around you in a circle, offering you the energy of loving comfort. Each amplifies the highest energy of love to soothe

any pain in your heart, anything that has made you feel alone and isolated. You feel at peace, calm, and relaxed. Through the energy of love they emit, you feel more whole, complete, and stronger. Their soothing, comforting love has restored you. You may stay as long as you like. They want you to know you can come to them for comfort any time you think of them because they are always available.

Thank them for their care and love as you come back into the space where you began your journey.

You have done more than you know as you do this meditative practice. You are not only opening your heart, but you are benefiting your health and well-being, as you release any burden leading you to a more fulfilled and happier life

Thank you for making it this far!

I greatly appreciate the time you took to read my book. It means a lot to me, and I hope you have been helped on your journey to find peace and finally let go and feel freer.

If you have a minute, it will mean the world to me to read your honest feedback on Amazon.

Your review does wonders for the book and will help me offer the book to others who can be helped by reading it.

To leave a review, go to the sales page where you purchased the book on Amazon, scroll to the bottom where the reviews are, and on the left side you will see **'review this product'** and click on 'write a customer review.'

Thank you!

ABOUT THE AUTHOR

Author Darla Luz began a spiritual journey fourteen years ago that led her to write four books on Consciousness. Her first book, *the Heart of Attention,* reached bestseller status, in which she tells her story, the stress-filled negative event that was the catalyst for writing so that others could learn from her experience and apply it to their own life.

She is passionate about expanding and raising the consciousness of all who read her books, writing about it in an easy-to-understand way.

She describes Consciousness as simply living present, aware of your surroundings and your inner self *now in this moment.*

Living peacefully present and aware day to day, she says dissolves the suffering of inner conflict, emphasizing that it is really that simple.

However, she understands that it is not easy in a world that is more stressed and anxious than ever. For this reason, her books are filled with techniques and daily practices that help the reader let go of all inner conflict in the same moment they are at peace, present, and aware.

www.ingramcontent.com/pod-product-compliance
Lightning Source LLC
Chambersburg PA
CBHW071536040426
42452CB00008B/1037